New Directions for Young Adult Services

New
Directions
for
Young Adult
Services

EDITED BY

Ellen V. LiBretto

R. R. Bowker Company
New York and London, 1983

Published by R. R. Bowker Company
205 East Forty-second Street, New York, NY 10017
Copyright © 1983 by Xerox Corporation
All rights reserved
Printed and bound in the United States of America

Library of Congress Cataloging in Publication Data
Main entry under title:

New directions for young adult services.

    Includes index.
    1. Libraries, Young people's—Addresses, essays,
lectures. 2. Young adults—Books and reading—
Addresses, essays, lectures. 3. Youth—Books and
reading—Addresses, essays, lectures. 4. Public
libraries—Aims and objectives—Addresses, essays,
lectures. I. LiBretto, Ellen V.
Z718.5.N48 1983   025.5′27762′6   83-11752
ISBN 0-8352-1684-5

Contents

Preface

New Directions for Young Adult Services is intended for young adult librarians, young adult consultants and coordinators, media services librarians, library administrators, library school professionals, and other librarians concerned with the future of public library services for teenagers. Library service to teenagers in the public library is in jeopardy. Chronic funding problems leave many libraries and library systems searching for new directions to serve the needs of teenagers. The teen years are a time of transition and struggle for identity. In reflection, services for teenagers in the public library are also in transition while the profession is experiencing the growing pains of a technological revolution. It is a good time for trainers of young adult specialists and for practitioners to consider the impact of the following essays on their own situations.

The ideas discussed in this collection should offer guidance to those concerned with the future of teenage services. The public library must never lose sight of the patron who will soon become a voter and will enter into the mainstream of American society. The reshaping of library services for the teenager involves more than the purchase of books. At a time when the nation's illiteracy rate is rising, while the population is aging, public libraries must take time to reassess the services needed and to examine their impact on the teenage population. Libraries have always managed to deliver services using limited resources, but now if services for teenagers are to be sustained and rejuvenated, difficult choices must be made about the kinds of services chosen in order to assure for the young adult a fair share of these library resources.

This collection of essays comprises the work of contributors from a broad range of backgrounds within the library community and from support positions in the information field. They have drawn from their own experiences as librarians, library educators, and authors concerned with the future of library services to teenagers.

The introduction by the editor, Ellen V. LiBretto, places the young adult specialty in a management context, drawing upon the professional experiences of young adult librarians who benefited from the varied work experiences learned as YA librarian practitioners. Subsequent chapters are arranged into four parts beginning with "New Directions." In Chapter 1, which deals with nonprint media, Patricia Mackey and Ellin Chu, librarians with extensive experience in the selection of nonprint materials, stress the use of film and video as an entity in itself and as a distinct service of the public library. A list of film and video sources is appended to the chapter. In Chapter 2, "Microcomputers for Young Adults," Bob Smith and Ken Katona present the microcomputer as a vehicle for the YA librarian to lead the way in technology and as a natural tie-in for school/public library relations. They cover both the traditional aspects of technology, as in film and video programming, and also suggest the limitless uses of the microcomputer. With Chapter 3, John Cunningham offers a roundup of collection development and program ideas in "Library Services for Non–English-Speaking Youth" and gives examples on how librarians can deal with large segments of the population for whom English is a second language. In Chapter 4, "Youth Participation in Library Decision Making," Jana Varlejs shows how the aim of youth participation is to give young adults a chance to plan and direct activities that have an impact on others and to learn from the experience by having youth serve on youth advisory boards, library boards, and other decision-making bodies. Chapter 5 details how the editor's experience with merchandising library collections has become a key to the use of the whole collection, with particular emphasis on the benefits of merchandising techniques for young adult librarians and their teenage constituents.

Part II focuses on the changing literature developed for young adults. In Chapter 6, George Sullivan's "Writing for Young Adults" outlines the broad range of YA books he has written and explains his reasons for contributing to the genre. In Chapter 7, "The Trappings of Morality," Marilyn Kaye presents the evolution of the teenage romance novel from the

early message-laden books of the 1950s and 1960s to today's in-
formation-oriented books promoting freedom of choice. In
Chapter 8, Nat Hentoff in "Censorship Did Not End at Island
Trees" eloquently cites the difficult circumstances in which
many librarians find themselves when under the gun of censorship. Hentoff offers support and guidance to those librarians
who work in an environment where their collections come
under attack by a censor or censoring group. Rhonna Goodman
brings Part II to a close by stating in Chapter 9 that the
booktalk, although the most traditional method for focusing
classroom interest on books, is still very much alive in teenage
services. She offers concrete advice on how to develop public
library/school connections.

In Part III the contributors express concern that the public library should continue to occupy a source of leadership in the
community. In Chapter 10, Evie Wilson's "The Librarian in the
Youth Services Network" expresses strong feelings that those
librarians who attempt to deliver services to teenagers must
become involved in other agencies both nationally and locally,
so that library services to teens can be integrated with other
grass-roots community services. In Chapter 11, Patricia R.
Allen in "Toward Meeting the Information Needs of Young
People in New York City" describes the essential resources
needed to provide teenagers with adequate information services. A new service to teenagers designed to provide pre-em-
ployment and college guidance information, as discussed in
Chapter 12, "Learner's Advisory Services for Young Adults" by
Emma Cohn, gives a blueprint for libraries wanting to develop a
special collection of college and career selection aids, culled
from an existing library collection. Essential and useful print
and nonprint materials are listed in an appendix to the chapter.
In Chapter 13, Joan Neumann discusses the INTERSHARE
Network in "Library Resource Sharing for Youth." How to
define and create YA information networks, and the development of systems for interlibrary loan and other forms of
resource sharing for youth are addressed. In Chapter 14, "Col-
lege/Library Cooperation," Bruce Shuman sums up how a
library system and a college joined financial contacts and
talents to develop a unique urban library with an emphasis on
teenage services.

Part IV demonstrates the need for strong professional train-
ing of YA specialists at the professional and preservice levels.
Joan Atkinson writes in Chapter 15 of the perilous position the
YA course has in the library education curriculum and argues

for its continued survival. In Chapter 16 Evelyn Shaevel outlines, in "ALA, YASD, and the Young Adult Librarian," the part that the Young Adult Services Division of ALA can play in offering training, continuing education, and support to the YA librarian. Bruce Daniels in Chapter 17, "The Leadership of the State Library Agency in Young Adult Services," suggests how the state library can become the focal point for measuring and advocating current services and can help find ways to direct funds for additional and enhanced services.

Following the last chapter are two appendixes, "Guidelines for Youth Participation in Library Decision Making" and "Competencies for Librarians Serving Youth."

Many of the projects described by the contributors can enhance a library's teenage program or can stand alone as pilot projects in library systems. A number of the projects—in particular, developing learner's advisory services, teen advisory boards, merchandising, booktalking, and film and video showings—can be implemented with little or no funds by redeploying materials to enhance collections or services designed for young adults.

Cooperative projects can be troublesome and costly. However, developments in library technology and in particular the use of the microcomputer can facilitate the individual library's ability to meet many resource sharing, community information, and bibliographic needs of their young adult patrons. For non–English-speaking teenagers, efforts must be made to acquire appropriate materials.

Services for teenagers should not be based on the popular notion of doing more with less, but rather on accommodating the needs of teenagers by taking a careful look at the available staff, materials, and technology, so that a new direction in service patterns for teenagers integrated into the total public library mission statement can be developed.

I am indebted to the contributors, who shared their ideas and enthusiasm with hope for the future of the YA renaissance. I would like to thank my friends, family, and professional colleagues, who waited patiently while the work was in progress, and my editor, Joanne O'Hare, whose patience and direction helped shape the scope of this book.

Ellen V. LiBretto

Contributors

Patricia R. Allen is Information Specialist, Service Agency Inventory System, The Greater New York Fund/United Way.

Joan L. Atkinson is Associate Professor, Graduate School of Library Service, University of Alabama, University, AL.

Ellin Chu is Young Adult Consultant, Monroe County Library System, Rochester, NY.

Emma Cohn is former Assistant Coordinator, Young Adult Services, The New York Public Library.

John Cunningham is Regional Branch Librarian, Free Library of Philadelphia.

Bruce Daniels is Deputy State Librarian for Rhode Island.

Rhonna Goodman is Young Adult Specialist, Borough of Staten Island, The New York Public Library.

Nat Hentoff is a prolific writer on censorship and other issues.

Ken Katona is Assistant, Audio Visual Department, Cuyahoga County Public Library, Cleveland, OH.

Marilyn Kaye is Assistant Professor, Division of Library and Information Science, St. John's University, Jamaica, NY.

Ellen V. LiBretto is Young Adult Consultant, Queens Borough Public Library, Jamaica, NY.

Patricia Mackey is Audiovisual Consultant, Monroe County Library System, Rochester, NY.

Joan Neumann is Executive Director, New York Metropolitan Reference and Research Library Agency (METRO).

Bruce A. Shuman is Associate Professor, Graduate School of Library and Information Studies, Queens College, Flushing, NY.

Evelyn Shaevel is Executive Director, Young Adult Services Division, American Library Association.

Bob Smith is Automated Circulation System Coordinator, Cuyahoga County Public Library, Cleveland, OH.

George Sullivan is the author of more than 100 books for children and young adults.

Jana Varlejs is Director of Professional Development Studies, Graduate School of Communication, Information and Library Studies, Rutgers University, New Brunswick, NJ.

Evie Wilson, formerly Young Adult Services Specialist, Tampa-Hillsborough County (FL) Public Library System, is now Legislative Aide to Florida State Senator Betty Castor.

Introduction

Public library work is in a state of flux. Hard economic times combined with the library's entree into the technological arena, with emphasis on the management skills needed to administer public services in libraries, have led many young adult librarians to believe that library service to teenagers is a dead-ended career path.

Mid-career YA library staff can recite chapter and verse from professional biographies of those youth service librarians who were the pathbreakers in library service to teenagers. Marked with great pride in our professional history is their rise to coordinating, academic, and upper management positions. Upward mobility is a vital professional consideration among entry level library staff who detect early those staffing positions that display a greater range and experience needed for advancement. Young adult service is still, as the articles in this collection depict, an area of library work that has defied tradition, choosing instead to project a maverick role in the profession.

Recently, librarians with strong backgrounds in young adult services were asked to describe the professional skills they developed as young adult librarians that were essential to their movement into middle management positions. Following are some of their responses.

Mel Rosenberg, Coordinator YA Services, Los Angeles Public Library, listed the skills he felt to be essential as "Excellent book and other materials knowledge that is continuously broadened and deepened. Continuous high level communication with administrative front line staff and with one's peers at the same level as well. The ability to write and speak clearly and well. The ability to assess trends and to make constructive use of them to be imaginative, imaginative, imaginative!"

Penny Jeffrey, whose early experience was as Young Adult Specialist, Office of Young Adult Services, The New York Public Library, noted these activities: "Selling the library and the materials and services it has to offer by speaking to classes in schools and classes visiting the library. Reading as many books as possible, including ones kids like, to learn what attracts them and how to pick new ones. Paying close attention to popular music, for example, listening to local radio stations, reading *Billboard*, checking record charts. Learning the basics of YA programming and being alert to current interests."

Jack Forman was formerly YA Services/Branch Director, Free Public Library of Woodbridge, New Jersey. He stated: "Booktalking experience helps to develop public speaking skills. Reference service makes one aware of the public's informational needs and teaches one a method of eliciting this information. Working with staff on sensitizing them to YA library needs and behavioral expectations of teenagers gives one a feeling of what it's like to create miracles."

For Marion Carter, Agency Head, YA Services, Salt Lake City Public Library, Utah, essential skills involved "Experience as a YA librarian in lobbying for YA services, learning about the budget process, [and] working with the media."

Christy Tyson, YA Services, Coordinator, Spokane Public Library, Spokane, Washington, said: "Specific skills honed from YA librarian training [include]public speaking, staff training, developing and coordinating committees, [and] broad knowledge of libraries and YA services beyond knowledge of the literature."

Ma'lis Wendt, who gained early experience as Assistant Director, Office of Special Services, The New York Public Library, described four essential areas: "(1) Programming skills, including planning, interviewing, and doing booktalks, which prepared me for public presentations. (2) Outreach projects — with community contacts, dealing with other agencies and bureaucracy. (3) Collection development for young adults means that you have to read widely in juvenile literature as well as young adult and adult books. (4) Attitude and outlook — working with young adults almost automatically means being open to all kinds of interests, behavior, and ideas. Adolescence is a period of transition and the young adult librarian learns to cope with the changes in teens and therefore in staff and in other public."

Susan B. Madden was formerly Institutional Librarian, King County Juvenile Court, Seattle, Washington. For her, essential skills involved "Designing youth surveys to give information about YA program effectiveness and to allow for change; staff supervision, scheduling, learning to understand staffing needs. A knowledge of adolescent psychology, dealing with the problem patron and volunteers, and staff evaluations add to good personnel management practices."

The successful completion of these wide-ranging skills in YA work enabled the respondents in the survey to advance to middle management positions. Within the framework of these positions, they are using these skills to facilitate the origination and growth of YA services in varied settings.

Following are some highlights of the experiences of these same respondents in their work as middle managers today. They also make note of the job variety that has enabled them to expand their knowledge of library operations.

Mel Rosenberg of the Los Angeles County Library System points up what he regards as important: "The ability to make quick decisions when necessary and slow ones when necessary, and the gift to know when each is required. This takes practice. The ability to organize, plan, carry out, and *complete* projects so that they look easy and the seams don't show. The ability to turn criticism, no matter the degree of negativity, into positive ideas, goals, and tangible projects. Some experiences here [that have been helpful]: City-wide poetry and drawing contests, 1976–1981; a variety of publications: the annual book list, the *MINDGRABBERS* book-list/book-cover; attractive and useful YA-oriented subject bibliographies, a program resource file. Teaching the YA course at USC and California State University, Long Beach. This last definitely causes one's ideas of service and materials selection to jell. Finally, and this is major, the ability to know if the middle-management level, which allows one to influence administration and still remain in close touch with materials selection and services, is what one most wants instead of the often lucrative but sometimes sterile ascent into the administrative empyrean. It will come up and come up and keep coming up."

Penny Jeffrey, now Regional Head, YA Services, Parma Regional Library, Cuyahoga County Library System, Ohio, cautions: "Learn the rules of your institution, procedures, etc., by studying whatever guides it publishes and taking whatever inhouse seminars are given. This is important—go with the program and if you want to change something, present a clear description of how your suggestions would work. Make use of state and national library conference programs on management skills. No matter what you set out to do, plan ahead. There will always be surprises, but many wrinkles can be anticipated. Don't be afraid to ask your supervisor and other colleagues for specific advice and assistance. It is flattering to be asked."

Jack Forman, from Mesa College Library in San Diego, mentions: "Committee work both inhouse and service on committees in professional associations (regional, state, national). LSCA grant proposal writing, implementation, and reporting. Workshop leader in book and film reviewing. Creating annotated book and film lists for teenagers and for staff who work with them. Getting involved with internal politics—convincing administrative staff and colleagues to support what you want."

Marion Carter, now YA Coordinator at the Salt Lake City Public Library, highlights these activities: "Staff development role in planning, developing, and addressing staff training seminars. Booktalking and storytelling lecture/demonstration led to gaining confidence in public speaking. Guest lecturing at colleges and universities on library youth services. Active in censorship and intellectual freedom issues and debates. Active membership in community board affiliations, 4H Advisory Board, and Muscular Dystrophy Educational Board."

Christy Tyson of the Spokane Public Library, lists: "Coordinating projects with other departments, for example, negotiating for computer access to YA paperbacks. Serving on community boards (YWCA, Planned Parenthood). Additional course work in management, especially budgeting. Participating in task forces on long-range planning, researching video, revising general library procedures, etc."

Ma'lis Wendt, now Assistant Coordinator, Donnell Library Center, The New York Public Library, says: "Young Adult was my first specialty, but I quickly was involved in work with all age levels. Young Adult training experience is very helpful because a good young adult librarian draws upon materials from both children and adult collections to serve young adults. Working with young adults also seems to generate excitement, enthusiasm, and a willingness to try out new ideas, new materials, and new media. My work with videotape workshops for teenagers led to my appointment to The New York Public Library Non-Print Media Committee and to other such projects and to my being noticed by the administration. Other committee work for Office of Young Adult Services was also helpful. Working with LSCA (Library Services and Construction Act) projects and grants gave me budget experience, which I have used in many different areas. Organizational skills and public relations work were also areas that I first used as a young adult librarian. I have been fortunate to have had a wide variety of work experiences, in several different systems, and within The New York Public Library in different administrative settings, all of which gave me broad and in-depth experience. And, of course, ALA/YASD involvement has also been important."

Susan B. Madden, today Coordinator of Young Adult Services, King County Library System, lists: "Community liaison with schools and other youth-serving agencies including conference presentations, booklist production, writing for newsletters, journals, etc. Membership in professional organizations, regional, state, and national. Involvement in organizations against censorship. Participating in Washington Career Assessment Center for Librarians—assessed management skills. Additional training in assertiveness training, time management, video production, interviewing techniques, and computer applications."

The skills that these librarians have mastered are all by-products of the design and implementation of many of the ideas and projects compiled in *New Directions for Young Adult Services*. These skills are transferable and essential for any librarian's continuing professional development.

Through the process of completing the projects in this book, not only will awareness and use of the public library increase for the teenager, but these experiences in managing the projects will stretch and develop the YA librarian's professional competencies in those critical areas needed for transition to the managerial role in the public library.

I
New Directions

1

Nonprint Media: New Formats and New Uses for Today's Teens

PATRICIA MACKEY and ELLIN CHU

In 1972, a thirteen-year-old boy went to see the feature film *Slaughterhouse Five*. Immediately afterward, he went to the public library, where he borrowed every book he could find by Kurt Vonnegut, searched through volumes on World War II to piece together historical accounts about the bombing of Dresden, and checked out recordings by Glenn Gould (who had played Bach on the film's sound track). Did *Slaughterhouse Five* change this young man's life? Did it make a reader out of a nonreader? Turn a dropout into a self-motivated student? Create an appreciation for classical music? Absolutely not! This multitalented teenager had studied music since the age of six, and throughout his school life remained at the top of his class. For him, films provided wonderful experiences, enriched his imagination, stimulated his curiosity, and enlarged his perspective.

Since the early 1950s librarians have known that films can have these same effects on almost anyone—that films are potentially the most powerful programming tool available to them. Who can resist the magical combination of big screen, dark room, larger-than-life images and the closeness of shadowy strangers? After three decades, trends indicate that film as a medium has not lost its usefulness or effectiveness and has survived the newer technologies as well. Aside from a film's ability to hold its audience spellbound, there are basically two other reasons why films endure: the infinite variety of excellent material available and the wide range of multipurpose programs that can be developed using films as a focus.

Fiction Films

Hollywood created, and television has perpetuated, the myth that film is a dramatic, not a photographic, medium; therefore films must tell stories. Librarians tend to program fiction films because they are both the most familiar and the most readily accepted by general audiences, including teenagers. We all like to become emotionally involved with the people and the events flickering on the screen; we like to laugh, cry, and get scared.

But these films can do more than entertain and tease our senses. Such films as *Tex, Snowbound,* and *Summer of My German Soldier* show teenagers coping with disastrous situations involving loyalty and survival—and have the added advantage of being based on young adult novels. *Brian's Song* (a 1972 made-for-television feature) remains a favorite with teens who respond immediately to the themes of friendship and death in the dramatized biography of Brian Piccolo, the Chicago Bears halfback who died of cancer at age twenty-six.

Filmmakers frequently use a dramatic setting as a palatable way to explore problems: *Francesca Baby* deals with a parent's alcoholism; in *Eugenie,* the young heroine makes a traumatic transition from girl to woman; and the teenage hero of *A Special Gift* finds that his manhood is in question because he wants to be a ballet dancer. Not all filmmakers use a serious approach or a story line to identify teenage concerns: *Making Points* makes its points with a satirical look at stereotyped male/female roles, and *Dear Diary* and *Am I Normal?* are *not* your standard self-conscious sex-education films, but all three provoke lively discussion as well as laughter from a young adult audience.

As a literary form, the short story is most easily transferred from printed page to 16mm film. Ranging from the light-hearted James Thurber tale *Mr. Preble Gets Rid of His Wife* (a farcical version of marital-sexual politics) to Susan Glaspell's *A Jury of Her Peers* (a somber story of guilt and guiltlessness in a sparse turn-of-the-century farm setting), there are countless examples of outstanding works in the genre. Some of the best are from the American short-story series distributed by Perspective, such as *Bernice Bobs Her Hair* (F. Scott Fitzgerald), in which an ugly duckling becomes a flirtatious vamp, or *Paul's Case* (Willa Cather), a story of adolescent defiance. *The Veldt* is only one of several successful Ray Bradbury works that dramatizes the ironies and dreadful consequences of living in a technological society. Often overlooked, *A Mother's Tale*, from James Agee's powerful allegory, is a stunning masterpiece about personal responsibility and the devastating effects of conformity, using a family of cows as protagonists.

Documentary Films

Whereas fiction films rearrange imagined events into controlled sequences, the documentary film takes real lives, information, and actual events and rearranges reality into a well-ordered whole. *The Life and Times of Rosie the Riveter, Union Maids,* and *The Day after Trinity* are masterful examples of film used for documenting history. *Rosie* follows the rise and fall of millions of "Rosies," women who worked in skilled industrial trades during World War II; *Union Maids* is a chronicle of a 1930s labor movement; and *The Day after Trinity* traces the career of Robert Oppenheimer as director of the atomic bomb project.

Using subjects more personal in scale, both *Who Are the De Bolts?* and its sequel, *Stepping Out: The De Bolts Grow Up,* reveal a remarkable, if not unique, family whose warmth and determination strike responsive chords in young adult audiences. *Quilts in Women's Lives* is an irresistible film for all ages, less about a traditional craft and more concerned with human values. An upbeat documentary about an inner-city teenage girls' track team, *The Flashettes*, speaks directly to this age group, as does the more starkly tragic *Mom, I Want to Come Home Now*, a dark view of juvenile prostitution. Most of these documentaries were not produced with a young adult

audience in mind, but they make passionate, personal statements, which teenagers know are steps beyond mere journal-
istic reportage.

Experimental Films

Films do not work miracles, but many *are* miracles—those
magical films that dazzle and astound and display the technical virtuosity that makes film a unique medium. For many
years, librarians felt that the personal, experimental film was
too obscure for use in young adult programming. (These were
the films we kept for ourselves!) But use of these films on cable
television as Home Box Office (HBO) shorts and extensive programming on the rock station MTV Music Television have
given us a new category for young adult viewing.

Computer-generated films like *Lapis* and visual fireworks
like *Allures* no longer mystify; *Off/On* has lost its threat.
Always accessible, animation and change-speed techniques
have delighted teenagers who often ask for an immediate rerun
when the pixilated *Wizard of Speed and Time* and *Vicious
Cycles* are shown. The double sound track of *Frank Film* may
confuse us, but teens love the visual feast of this brilliant mon-
tage. Satire goes hand in hand with animation, exemplified by
the now-classic *Hardware Wars* and the lesser known *Hank,
the Cave Peanut*.

Teenagers are fascinated by technique and also like to see
films made by their peers. *Animation Pie* combines both interests, presenting an array of animation styles in a sampling of
teen-made shorts. Perhaps the best known survivor of the latter genre, the live-action *That Rotten Tea Bag*, has remained
popular for over a decade of young adult programming.

Limitations of Film

Now for the bad news about film: The 16mm film is still the
single most expensive item libraries own. This fact alone
greatly restricts the range and quantity of titles available to
young adult librarians.

Ideally, films should be previewed before programs are
planned, but this is a time-consuming process, often compli-
cated by the library's booking system. (Films must be booked

in advance, making it difficult to have a spontaneous film showing.) We are also competing for our audience's time—the audience that once eagerly rushed to library programs may now rush more eagerly to the videogame scenes, or may stay at home to be enthralled by HBO, Cinemax, Showtime, and a multitude of television channels.

Although film, for the most part, is a passive medium with few allowances for interaction, teenagers can be involved in selecting films for their own programs and discussions can be included as part of the program event. But teenagers like to *produce*, to create their own materials, to be and see themselves. Enter video!

Video

Is video the answer? These are the questions: Are you looking for a device that allows teenagers to express themselves through a combination of visuals and sound and that can also include writing, research, dramatics, plus teamwork? A tool that provides instant playback, living color, and a capability for program exhibition? A technology recognized and accepted by almost everyone, regardless of age, background, or economic level?

Beginning with the black and white reel-to-reel portapack and continuing most recently with small color cameras, light-weight videocassette tape decks, and reasonable prices, video is an ideal means for self-expression. An introductory hands-on training session usually results in instant producers. Teens have created library orientation programs, recorded local history, turned original stories into tapes, and presented provocative discussions through video.

In summer 1982, a city-sponsored youth project allowed the Rochester (New York) Public Library to hire a team of high school and college teenagers to produce a documentary tape on the cultural assets of the local area. The result was an in-depth forty-minute production, conceived, scripted, shot, and edited by the student group. Local community organizations and industries are now using the tape because it presents such a comprehensive view of varied cultural resources, effectively organized into a single program. There are many success stories like this!

Community access cable is a natural outlet for in-house pro-

ductions, and often librarians encourage teenagers to participate regularly in library cable activities. Because many schools
have video production equipment plus student talent, video
has the added advantage of providing a means for cooperative
ventures between schools and public libraries.

The value and uses of video, of course, go beyond in-house
taping. Prerecorded tapes (usually current feature films) are the
basis for popular lending collections, but are not the ideal programming source, since copyright laws and the physical size of
a television monitor limit public exhibition. Trends in both
licensing (for exhibition purposes) and development of large-
screen video projection systems may change this.

But don't overlook independent video productions as a viable
source. Tapes like *Pick Up Your Feet* (a dazzling display of
double-dutch jump rope) and *Just Another Missing Kid* (a spell-
binding Canadian documentary about the fate of a teenager en
route to California and winner of the 1983 Academy Award for
best documentary) are only two examples of the outstanding
tapes suitable for young adult programs. The trend is for most
recent 16mm film to become available in video formats. Based
on the theory "if you can't join 'em, beat 'em at their own
game," a few libraries are now offering videogames to their
teenage public. You reach them where they live!

Recordings

We all know that teenagers also live with recordings: LPs,
cassettes, and 45s. Long-playing records found a permanent
place in libraries more than thirty years ago; cassettes have
been established since the late 1960s. But 45s (the current "Top
40") are now recognized as useful for young adult oriented collections as well. The instant accessibility and low cost, combined with minimum cataloging and processing, make this format a kind of "paperback" of recordings. The recent growth of
books-on-cassettes has added another dimension to young
adult recording collections, with books ranging from the peren-
nial romantic favorite *Rebecca* to science fiction classics by
Arthur Clarke and Isaac Asimov.

In Retrospect

One of the advantages of young adult work is that your patrons
always outgrow you, making way for new faces, new interests,

new challenges. Remember the thirteen-year-old Vonnegut fan at the beginning of this chapter? He is now an adult of twenty-three. In ten years, he witnessed the birth of the home computer, the videogame, and the videodisc. In fact, he called the other day to talk about his new job involving a videodisc retrieval system. He was also very excited about a wonderful film he'd just seen again for the third time. It's called *Slaughterhouse Five*.

Filmography

Entries list title, producer/director, running time, year of release, and distributor.

Allures. Jordan Belson, 8 min., 1961, Pyramid.

Am I Normal? Debra Franco & David Shepard, 24 min., 1979, New Day.

Animation Pie. Robert Bloomberg, 25 min., 1974, Film Wright.

Bernice Bobs Her Hair. Joan Micklin Silver, 48 min., 1977, Perspective.

Brian's Song. P. J. Witt, 75 min., 1972, LCA.

The Day after Trinity: J. R. Oppenheimer and the Atomic Bomb. Jon Else, 88 min., 1980, Pyramid.

Dear Diary. Debra Franco & David Shepard, 25 min., 1980, New Day.

Eugenie. Susan Sussman, 16 min., 1977, Phoenix.

The Flashettes. Bonnie Friedman, 20 min., 1977, New Day.

Francesca Baby. Larry Elikann, 46 min., 1976, Disney.

Frank Film. Frank Morris, 9 min., 1973, Pyramid.

Hank, the Cave Peanut. Ron McAdow, 15 min., 1974, Beacon Films.

Hardware Wars. Ernie Fosselius, 13 min., 1978, Pyramid.

A Jury of Her Peers. Sally Heckel, 30 min., 1980, Texture.

Just Another Missing Kid. John Zaritsky, 87 min., 1981, CBS.

Lapis. James Whitney, 10 min., 1967, Creative Film Society.

The Life and Times of Rosie the Riveter. Connie Field, 65 min., 1980, Clarity.

Making Points. Charlotte Zwerin, Ellen Hovde, Muffie Meyer, 11 min., 1980, Direct Cinema Ltd.

Mr. Preble Gets Rid of His Wife. Ellen Hovde, Muffie Meyer, 17 min., 1980, Direct Cinema Ltd.

Mom, I Want to Come Home Now. Fleming Fuller, 57 min., 1979, Chronicle.

A Mother's Tale. Rex Victor Goff, 18 min., 1975, LCA.

Off/On. Scott Bartlett, 10 min., 1967, NET.

Paul's Case. Lamont Jackson, 54 min., 1979, Perspective.

Pick Up Your Feet: The Double Dutch Story. Skip Blumberg, 30 min., 1981, Skip Blumberg. Video only.

Quilts in Women's Lives. Pat Ferrero, 28 min., 1980, New Day.

Slaughterhouse Five. George Roy Hill, 104 min., 1972, Universal. (16mm, rental only)

Snowbound. Andrew Young, 33 min., 1978, LCA.

A Special Gift. Martin Tahse Productions, 47 min., 1979, Time-Life.

Stepping Out: The De Bolts Grow Up. Jon Else, 52 min., 1980, Pyramid.

Summer of My German Soldier. Michael Tuchner, 98 min., 1978, LCA.

Tex. Tim Hunter, 103 min., 1982, Disney. (not yet available in 16 mm.)

That Rotten Tea Bag. Andy Gurlan, 4 min., 1971, Youth Film Distribution Center.

Union Maids. Julia Reichert, 49 min., 1975, New Day.

The Veldt. Dianne Haak, 24 min., 1979, BFA.

Vicious Cycles. Jansen Menville & Brain, 7 min., 1969, Pyramid.

Who Are the De Bolts? John Korty, 72 min., 1977, Pyramid.

Wizard of Speed and Time. Mike Jittlov, 3 min., 1979, Pyramid.

2

Microcomputers for Young Adults: They'll Love Every Byte!

BOB SMITH and KEN KATONA

Microprocessors—they are everywhere, from our wristwatches, to our automobiles, to our microwave ovens, to our security systems, to our television sets. The basic personal computer today offers computing power unimaginable only five or ten years ago. Vast arrays of tubes and wires that used to take up huge amounts of space have now been compressed into the size of a portable typewriter. Languages have been developed with the user in mind to enable this computing power to be within the reach of most people. Touch-sensitive screens and light pens that take advantage of pictographic applications of response rather than the printed word also are in wide use. Continuing development and marketing of speech synthesizers for commonly distributed personal computing systems will conceivably eliminate the need for even pictorial representations for interaction between user and machine. The mere ability to vocalize within a computer's specialized vocabulary will be the only requirement.

But what does all this modern technology have to do with library services for young adults? Actually a great deal. In the

11

1980s, the public library has a unique opportunity to offer information and to assist in demonstrating the information, education, and recreation capabilities of microcomputer technology.

Microcomputers for Education and Recreation

Teens are extremely aware of one of the more successful applications of the microprocessor today: videogames. Arcade
games are everywhere, from bowling alleys, to shopping malls,
to pizza shops. Personal computers have many of the same
game-playing capabilities that arcade videogames have, and as
classrooms and media centers acquire micros, a highly requested application is bound to the the playing of videogames.
Taking advantage of the novelty, colors, sounds, and excitement generated by videoprogrammers, educational software
firms have developed instructional programs for schools using
many of the same features to attract adolescents.

What has this done to education? Many teachers feel that attendance is better when microcomputers are used in formerly
dull drill activities. Also, microcomputers can free teachers
from many of the routine record-keeping chores. Students have
the opportunity to learn at their own pace, with truly constant
attention by an infinitely patient tutor: the micro. State-of-the-
art programs allow learners to progress through complex learning mazes at perfectly matched, individualized rates. All the
while, the computer is keeping score and offering immediate
feedback: Well-chosen praise for correct responses and keys to
the correct answers are essential ingredients for the reluctant
learner.

Can these educationally sound activities be effectively util-
ized in the media center and the public library? The answer is a
resounding "Yes." Innovative programs, with the informational
support of well-established book and nonbook materials, are
being tried all over the country. State media associations with
production contests for students (traditionally for art, sculp-
ture, poetry, and photography) now include sections for
original student-authored computer programs. Public libraries
are having computer fairs and programming contests, and
many are adding micros as an integral part of their service. Use
by young adults ranges from amusement to the word processing of term papers and reports. Instructional programs are

being added to audiovisual collections as would be filmstrips and cassette tapes. Readily available programs help to learn a foreign language, test mathematical relationships, graph quadratic equations, analyze the difficulty level of a text, and chart stocks to illustrate business concepts.

In the area of recreation, a whole new group of materials is flourishing: adventure-type computer games. These are not comparable to videogames, nor are they necessarily educational. They do, however, test the player's logic and memory against ghosts, criminals, or fantastic beasts, dragons, and the like. Adventure simulations also can be based on real events, such as "Eastern Front 1941," in which the player manipulates armies, supplies, and war-game strategies during World War II, or a wagon train trek across the pioneer frontier toward the Pacific Northwest.

A Few Sample Programs

Experiences with microcomputers vary considerably from library to library, as demonstrated by these examples from various Ohio libraries.

An elaborate program at the Lorain Public Library initially was funded through city block-grant funds. Monthly training sessions are provided, and a large collection of software is maintained for in-house use only. Game playing is limited to a few hours per week per person, and all age groups are using the computers enthusiastically.

In Fairfield County, Lancaster Public Library's LSCA grant provided the initial equipment. The young adults in the area were so excited about the prospects for computer use that they sponsored their own fund-raising activities to purchase additional software for the library's collection.

Cleveland Heights/University Heights Public Library also has a microcomputer available for public use in its Children's Room. The staff provides training sessions in elementary operation and BASIC language. No game playing is allowed.

One enterprising youth approached an adult librarian at the Orange Branch of the Cuyahoga County Public Library with an interesting proposition. The youth wondered if the librarian would like his name placed into a program that would have the computer generate a personalized, x-rated, pornographic adventure — with the librarian as the central character, of course!

Selecting the Equipment

No ideal configuration can be recommended to serve the needs of young adults, or of any other group for that matter. Selection of equipment must be a careful process, with special emphasis upon the tasks the computer equipment will be asked to perform. Even more frustrating for librarians, who continually read about the major technological changes occurring so rapidly, is the knowledge that what is purchased today will be replaced on the marketplace by a larger unit with more capabilities at less cost amazingly soon. However, that should not deter the acquisition of a microcomputer, because a tremendous amount of learning can be accomplished with any unit.

Although a blitz of advertising concerning low-end units has some of the general public believing that tremendous microcomputing power is available for under $200, it is highly improbable that a microcomputer of this price can fill the needs of a public library. Disk drives, quiet, reliable, and fast printers, as well as higher quality monitors, are all individually more costly than that figure. Surely recent prices for computer capacity have decreased, but the peripheral attachments (such as monitors, disk drives, printers, and interfaces) have remained relatively stable.

Some libraries have wisely explored intriguing options offered by enterprising entrepreneurs of the micro/tech world. Coin-operated combinations are offered by at least a handful of vendors; some even have an option to apply rental fees toward an eventual purchase. Although these offers enable great capabilities with little or no capital outlay (some even cover insurance costs), they bring up the question of provision of service at a cost—a sensitive issue traditionally avoided by libraries whenever possible. Pay access to a microcomputer would, in fact, simply restrict from access the economically disadvantaged groups that need it most to compete in today's marketplace. Clear goals of library service as stated in a board-approved policy statement should shed some light.

Following are some of the criteria that should be taken into consideration in the selection of equipment for young adult users:

1. Color, sound, and graphics
2. Upper- and lowercase characters
3. Compatibility with school equipment

4. Word-processing capability

5. Disk drive(s)

6. Printer of decent quality

7. Curriculum-based software

8. Tutorials on computer programming

9. Support of book and periodical materials

10. Recreational software

11. Availability of a resident authority

Obviously, many of these considerations relate directly to school applications. With this in mind, a public library just entering the microcomputer field or expanding an existing program might well contact the local school media specialist for information and recommendations. The library might also want to invite a core group of interested youth to assist not only in the equipment and software selection but also in the development of guidelines and regulations.

Installing and Supervising the Equipment

Once a microcomputer has been selected for the young adult area in the library, it is time to start carefully inspecting the environment in which it will be situated. The often overlooked electrical outlet is critical. Many existing outlets are not suitable, due to power surges within the circuit from other equipment. Separate circuits may be required for consistently reliable operation. Static electricity may also be a problem in buildings with certain types of carpeting and low-humidity combinations. The discharge of static electricty not only can cause loss of information on disks and cassettes but can actually do permanent damage to some components of the hardware itself. Special floor mats often are a reasonable solution to this problem.

Supervision of the equipment is a factor that should not be overlooked. A key ingredient to the success of most public library programs is the availability to the public of a resident expert on the library staff to answer the myriad questions about the operation and the potential of the microcomputer. Many librarians feel they need to take endless hours of programming courses at local community colleges to outperform the public.

The realities are that, for the most part, a very basic skill level is sufficient for the majority of public library applications. Furthermore, experts seem to appear out of the woodwork—from schools, from local commercial establishments, and from user groups (such as the Apple Corps, those who use Apple computer products)—to assist the library with more complex problems. In fact, a user group may be one of the most helpful organizations meeting in the community room of a public library. A high school teacher provides a weekly course on programming at the Orange Community Branch of the Cuyahoga County (Ohio) Public Library with the library's Apple II + and the TRS-80 micros. As important as supervision is, it does not necessarily imply detailed instruction in programming theory. The software is becoming more and more user-friendly; that is, it is easier to operate with lower and lower levels of computer literacy.

The equipment may be more useful on a rolling cart of some type, to be placed in certain areas of the building as needed and then rolled to more secure quarters for other periods. This also makes it possible for one microcomputer to serve several different purposes—for example, in the juvenile room for the preschoolers in the early afternoon, in the youth adult corner after school, and in the adult area for business applications and school assignments during the evening. The mornings can be made available for the staff to work on bibliographies, type reports on the word-processing program, analyze the bond issue surveys, and create mailing labels for a "Friends of the Library" campaign.

Do not forget to consider the noise levels, which may affect other library activities, when deciding on a location for the computer. All printers claim to be quiet, but few are. Groups of youth can get quite enthusiastic about their progress (or lack thereof) in writing a program or solving an adventure.

Policies for Equipment Use

Written routines for handling software, and for scheduling use of the equipment, need to be worked out before the equipment is installed for public use. Many libraries routinely allow the staff to use the micro for a period of time before the public is allowed access, in order to boost their confidence and skill level. The North Pulaski Branch of the Chicago Public Library has developed an interesting computer center approach. All equipment and software are offered for demonstration purposes only. This, of course, relieves the library of responsibility for any assumed guarantees on the part of the users in case of software failure, equipment malfunction, or simply the unavailability at times of the equipment. It is important to consider the perceived expectations of the public in formulating policies relating to computer use.

Limitations as to types of use at certain times of the day, or how much time per person per day or per week, also should be carefully considered. Some libraries limit game playing to only a certain amount of time per week. Writing a game program and playing a game are certainly not the same thing, and the supervisor should become somewhat familiar with what the users are attempting.

Scheduling microcomputer access provides equal opportunity for all who wish it, whether for programming or for recreation. Experience has shown that youth will come into the library before their scheduled time to use the library's book and periodical collections, even though they may not have done so in the past.

The Future

It is a fairly safe guess that in the future micros will be increasingly available to adolescents—in schools, at home, and in libraries. Summer computer camps are springing up and are quite popular. Several universities and colleges have issued requirements of student ownership of a microcomputer for entry as a freshman, and more and more high schools are requiring passing a computer literacy course for graduation.

Public schools are probably far ahead of public libraries in microcomputer usage. This, however, is an opportunity for public libraries to extend an open hand of cooperation. It is probably not realistic to expect that joint evaluation of programs and hardware can occur often, but a little public relations can go a long way. Local media specialists can be consulted before final selections are made and for tips on actual usage patterns.

As more and more libraries add microcomputers to their buildings, the future will see increased use by both the library and its patrons. Easily created and updated microcomputer files will replace several traditional library card files, such as ready-reference questions for school assignments, locally useful and "ephemeral" information, and information and referral (I&R) files.

The information-retrieval potential of microcomputers will expand their use by libraries. With a relatively small investment in equipment, a library can access major data bases throughout the country for informational and recreational needs. As cooperation between the school and the public library increases, perhaps shared data bases will evolve. A student may be able to access the school's computer by phone from the public library. Students will be able to complete school assignments with library resources, storing the results on a diskette to take to school or sending the results directly to the school's computer.

Electronic mail will allow classes to interact across the country, much as pen pals commonly do today. Not only will English composition and communication skills be developed, but computer skills as well.

It may be an unfamiliar world of librarianship ten or twenty-five years from now—a world in which the librarian is spending most of the time assisting patrons in a series of data base search strategies from a terminal. Books, periodicals, newspapers, movies, and other forms of information and entertainment will be accessible through the video screen. The terminal/telephone will be the center of activity, able to reach exotic sources of information in an instant, as well as do local shopping and banking. Paperback novels may be rare items in a paperless information society. Young adults of today will have great opportunities to experience the birth of future industries—right in their local public library!

Further Reading

Because of the extremely rapidly changing nature of information concerning microcomputers, the authors decided not to include a bibliography. Books and articles proliferate in the publishing world. Any list included here would be outdated by the time of publication and hence misleading. Many excellent periodicals exist, each with a special slant toward a specific reader group. New publications appear frequently, especially those dealing with specific models of computers.

Research the literature, especially library literature, for success stories upon which to model a program. Write or call for follow-up information and/or newer guidelines that may have been developed since the article appeared. Librarians throughout the country are more than willing to share their experiences.

3
Library Services for Non–English-Speaking Youth

JOHN CUNNINGHAM

Although services to young people have had a higher priority among libraries than have services to the non–English-speaking public, neither has received the attention it deserves. Focusing on such exotica as library services to non–English-speaking youth reveals even larger service gaps. Exceptions do exist however. There are libraries where a combination of administrative commitment and support, coupled with creative and energetic direct services staff, has produced significant contributions to a pioneering service.

In Support of Bicultural Staff

It was at the New Orleans Public Library (where my own first employment in a library occurred in 1972) that I first witnessed the development of a concerted effort to serve a non–English-speaking community. The library received Library Services and Construction Act (LSCA) funding for Project Jericho, a joint program by Orleans and St. Bernard parishes to knock down the invisible walls that kept the community's Spanish-speaking public from using the library. Administrative commitment was evident in the recognition of a need, in the support required to prepare for a grant, in recruiting a qualified staff to administer the project, in staff training, and I am glad to report, in continuing special services to the Spanish-speaking once the grant expired.

The staffing of Project Jericho made a lasting impression on me for the quality of leadership and dedication to service exhibited by the project director, Hilda ten Brink. Like myself, ten Brink was a graduate of the Latin American Studies master's program at Tulane University. Although neither of us had any library work experience, we received in-house training. In several months, we developed a collection, created a Spanish-language catalog, and opened the Spanish-language division to the public. Ten Brink soon had contacts in all the social, religious, civic, and cultural organizations within the Hispanic community. Project Jericho was a success.

Did I mention that ten Brink was originally from Cuba? I should have. Completely bilingual and bicultural, she was able to move with equal ease in the Hispanic community and within the library administration. Most important, she was part of the community the library sought to reach, not just during working hours but also in her private life. She not only knew contacts, she knew the contacts' cousins or where they were originally from and what work they did there. She was able to introduce the library into the intricate web of social relationships that exist in any community structure.

I have always thought that New Orleans Public Library showed good judgment by hiring a non-M.L.S. degreed person to coordinate its services to the Spanish-speaking. If it came to a decision of whether to hire an American librarian who knew some Spanish or a bilingual/bicultural Hispanic with some comparable level of education, I would choose the Hispanic. Project Jericho's federal funding ended, but many of the services continue through New Orleans Public Library's Foreign Language Division headed by Norka Diaz whose master's degree is in Spanish-language literature. When last I visited the Crescent City, Diaz was applying the skills she developed with Project Jericho to improving services for the recent influx of Vietnamese.

Of course, in the best of all possible worlds, there would be sufficient numbers of Puerto Rican, Russian, Vietnamese,

Korean, or Chinese librarians within our various ethnic communities to go around. Alas, even when such people exist, there are often bureaucratic roadblocks to hiring them. Not long ago I received a telephone call from a refugee resettlement agency asking if I could help a Cuban librarian with his job search. The person in question had headed the technical services division in one of Cuba's national libraries. He was fluent in Spanish, English, and German and had a reading knowledge of Russian. His application for several positions was turned down because his library degree was from the University of Havana, an institution not accredited by the American Library Association. This is certainly a fine example of bureaucratic myopia at its best.

Spanish is now our nation's second language. The last decade has seen the development of Spanish-language presses in the United States, as well as radio stations and a national Spanish-language television network, SIN, broadcasting to more than 200 locations. The Census Bureau estimates that by the year 2000, America's Hispanic community will be larger than our black community. Given the close cultural ties and geographic proximity of Mexico and Puerto Rico, use of Spanish will no doubt continue. Yet very few library schools have shown any leadership in the recruitment and training of professionals from Spanish-speaking communities.

Only the program at the University of Arizona, under the direction of Arnulfo Trejo, has made a lasting contribution by graduating several classes of librarians specifically trained in serving the Spanish-speaking community. Rutgers and Temple universities cooperated in a joint program to prepare bilingual librarians through Project LIBROS, but when federal funds ended after the first year, the program vanished. This small response from graduate library schools to our major linguistic minority community bodes ill for what smaller groups might expect.

English as a Second Language

Certainly the primary need of all non–English-speaking youth is to learn English and to be able to adapt to the dominant culture. When I discussed this essay with a friend who left Germany prior to World War II, he stressed over and over the importance of learning English. For him, it was the vehicle for education and for a job. The same is true today, more than forty years later. There is no escaping the fact that the ability to function within the dominant culture requires ability in English. What has changed in forty years is that there is today a growing recognition that new Americans need not abandon fluency in the original language or participation and pride in the original culture during the acculturation process. There is clearly a two-pronged message here for librarians: Help youth to learn English and to adjust to a new environment and provide recognition of the foreign culture through collection development and programming. In responding to these needs, the library can also act as an educational force in the community at large by informing Americans about their new neighbors.

Libraries have frequently responded to new immigrant populations by providing ESL (English as a Second Language) classes. Usually the library provides the meeting space and in cooperation with other agencies secures teachers and appropriate materials. Other cooperating agencies have included school districts, churches, social service agencies, and civic groups. Formal classes are but one response. Discussion groups also are very helpful in developing bilingual ability and require only a volunteer leader fluent in English. Most new immigrants remain isolated within their ethnic community and welcome the chance to practice conversation with native speakers. Most, too, are anxious to develop friendships with English-speaking Americans. Conversation classes and other library programs that bring limited English-speaking youth into contact with potential friends from the dominant culture help meet this need.

Collection Development in Foreign Languages

Libraries have also responded by purchasing easy readers written for adult learners. These materials have during recent years begun to stress life-coping skills and therefore are ideally suited to assist with the acculturation process. They frequently discuss the mechanics of finding a job, the intricacies of landlord-tenant relationships, the social service support structure, American law and the rights of all residents in America, and basic consumerism. Although most of these subjects appear to be adult rather than young adult in orientation, it is important to remember that in ethnic communities, it is frequently the young who learn English quicker and often serve as interpreters of language and culture to the older generation. Anyone who has worked with non–English-speaking communities is familiar with an adult seeking information or service through a son or daughter who speaks English. Three bibliographies that can assist librarians in developing collections of easily written adult materials are *Reader Development Bibliography* (New Readers Press, distributed by R. R. Bowker, 1982, $9.95); *Books for Adult New Readers* (Project LEARN, 2238 Euclid Avenue, Cleveland, OH 44118, 1983, $5); and *Bibliography of Basic Materials—Reading, English as a Second Language, Humanities* (Literacy Volunteers of America, 1980, $10).

Other collection development activities often have included the purchase and circulation of records and cassettes to learn English. A wide range of these materials is available and informed acquisition is not a particular problem. What is rare is for libraries to have language laboratories on site as part of their regular services. This is particularly strange given the modest investment required and the fact that in urban areas easily identified communities repeatedly serve as initial housing sites for new Americans. Need I add that these language labs could be used just as easily by Americans to learn foreign languages!

Recognition of non–English-speaking cultures can be provided by something as traditional as developing a collection of books, magazines, newspapers, and other materials in foreign languages. Librarians occasionally are too anxious to create roadblocks to the development of such collections: Where can I order these books? Who will catalog them? What can I do about the poor bindings? How can I tell what is appropriate—are some questions asked. Needless to say, any librarian worth her or his M.L.S. can find the answers. For advice on where to purchase materials, librarians can contact major metropolitan libraries with experience in service to non–English-speaking communities. The most comprehensive and dynamic collection building of foreign-language materials has been that of the North Carolina Foreign Language Center of the Cumberland County Public Library. It has materials in languages you may not have heard of and it serves the entire state through interlibrary loan and deposit collections. Another source of information on collection building in foreign languages is the National Clearinghouse for Bilingual Education (1555 Wilson Bou-

levard, Suite 605, Rosslyn, VA 22209; telephone 800-336-4560).
This agency maintains a computer data base with a wide variety of information relevant to those serving the non–English-
speaking community.

Programming for Youth

Programs offered by libraries seeking to reach out to non–
English-speaking youth have been as varied and creative as the
imagination of those who have offered them. The following
program examples were drawn from a survey conducted by
Adriana Tandler of the Queens Borough Public Library's New
Americans Project. Certainly one of the most imaginative and
creative service programs to ethnic communities is that ad-
ministered by the New Americans Project at the Queens
Borough Public Library in Jamaica, New York. Its philosophy is
that multicultural programs bring new people into the library,
exposing a new audience to the broad range of library services.
Among the programs that have been offered have been a
Chinese dance company, Greek poetry, plays in Spanish by the
Puerto Rican Traveling Theater, Slavic dancing, Andean
music, Russian folk singing, and Chinese shadow theater.
Queens Borough's foreign film festivals have included films in
Bengali, French, German, Greek, Hebrew, Italian, Japanese,
Korean, Polish, Russian, Spanish, and Yiddish—all with sub-
titles in English. The role of the family within ethnic commu-
nities is strong and the above-mentioned programs frequently
appeal to a broad range of ages.

Programming for youth can be grouped into several distinct
areas: social/recreational, arts and crafts, music, writing and
literature, cultural heritage, career education and job training,
and films. During adolescence the rise in the importance of the
peer group as an influential social dynamic can be recognized
in program development by catering to the recreation and
social interests of youth. The Los Angeles Public Library
(LAPL) has had several successful programs in this area for
Spanish-speaking youth, including a beauty club for girls, a
swimming club, and a library-sponsored basketball team.

The Club de Cultura y Belleza started when some girls com-
plained about not having anything to do. Sylvia Flores Johnson
of LAPL reported that twenty-five girls participated in the
weekly meetings held during the school year. There were guest
speakers on topics such as manicure, hairstyles, makeup, ward-
robe selection, sex hygiene and education, and other aspects of

good grooming. The sessions were informal and speakers were chosen on the basis of their ability to get the girls to ask questions and participate. At the end of each session, the young adult librarian would do a book talk on a topic of special interest to the girls. Halfway through the school year the club put on a show, which was a combination beauty contest and cultural heritage presentation.

The swimming club developed as a result of a complaint that area girls were not permitted to use the only local pool at the Los Angeles Times Boys Club. The young adult librarian intervened, got permission to use the boys' pool, and taught swimming to the girls once a week. Girls who couldn't afford the required swimming caps received free ones thanks to the library friends group Amigos de la Biblioteca.

The basketball team was developed to give some problem boys something constructive to do with their time. Uniforms were purchased by the Amigos de la Biblioteca, and tennis shoes were donated by local merchants. The team was coached by a library CETA worker. Although the boys never had any real competition, they had a good time, learned discipline, and advertised the library with their T-shirts emblazoned with the library name in bright red letters.

Arts and crafts programs can take various forms and provide an excellent opportunity to highlight and encourage ethnic art forms. Tie-dyeing, painting, printing, egg decoration, and decorative fabric work are but a few examples. Even when the library doesn't directly sponsor such activities, offering exhibit space and hosting receptions for artists can encourage community recognition of youth and foster appreciation and understanding of ethnic cultures. Various youth service agencies as well as public and private schools frequently foster artistic development among young people, and the young adult librarian who develops and maintains contact with these agencies will be able to offer library support for such programs.

Music and dance are among the most enduring of folk traditions and, like art, do not require foreign-language ability to be appreciated. Choruses, instrumentalists, and dance groups exist in most non–English-speaking communities and are available for library performances. Mai Chi Hua, a VISTA volunteer at the Free Library of Philadelphia, worked with a group of young people to present traditional dances as part of a Vietnamese New Year celebration. The bilingual chorus (Spanish/English) has likewise appeared in Free Library of Philadelphia programs to celebrate Three Kings Day. Miami-Dade Public Library regularly includes typical dances from various countries as part of its celebration of Hispanic Heritage Month.

But folk music need not be the sole focus of using music as a youth interest to encourage library use. A branch of the Los Angeles Public Library offers a piano for practice use. When a new piano was needed, the librarian, Mrs. Villegas, bought one on the installment plan and organized a fundraiser. With the help of the Conservatorio de Música, a piano recital was held at which the conservatory's best students performed. Among those in the recital was a student who later won a scholarship to study music at the Sorbonne in Paris. The library regularly makes available a wide selection of music for those studying the piano.

Of course, the more traditional domains of library interest, literature and writing, have not been neglected. Queens Borough Public Library secured the assistance of Argentine writer Luisa Valenzuela and ran a series of creative writing workshops for Spanish-speaking youth. At the end of the series, a booklet was published, "Viajes Imaginarios," which collected the best works of those in the group. A similar project was held in Russian. The Free Library of Philadelphia held a poetry workshop with Puerto Rican poet and dramatist Miguel Piñero, which attracted a bilingual audience of young people. There have also been programs with Piri Thomas and Nicholasa Mohr, Hispanic authors of books in English for young people; these programs brought in bilingual youth. At times, discussions in Spanish and English focused on the conflicts experienced by bilingual/bicultural youth. At Los Angeles Public Library a book review club was organized for young people from ages eleven to nineteen. Fifteen reviewers met every two weeks to advise the library in book selection. The program lasted for four months and could serve as a model for similar programs. Young adult librarians at the Los Angeles Public Library also regularly do book talks in Spanish during school visits.

Every culture has its own holidays and traditional celebrations, which libraries can use as vehicles to attract new Americans to the library. Hispanic Heritage Month, Vietnamese and Chinese New Years, independence celebrations, and birthdays of national or religious heroes are but a few examples of occasions when the library can recognize ethnic communities through special programs. I would offer only two caveats: First, ethnic holidays are celebrated by more than the library, and competition for an audience can be stiff at times. Second, re-cognition of ethnic communities only on special occasions can be construed as tokenism.

Finally, mention need be made of the importance of pro-grams that help orient non–English-speaking youth toward em-ployment opportunities and career planning. Of course, the schools must assume primary responsibility in this area, but here as elsewhere, it is imperative that young adult librarians maintain close contact with schools and work to supplement their offerings. Angelica Garcia, a YA librarian at LAPL de-veloped a very popular job information program series in English and Spanish. Guest speakers from the local employ-ment agency, high school counselors, and people working in popular fields were invited to participate in a weekly program during the summer. Brooklyn Public Library's El Centro Hispano de Información includes as part of its services an ac-tive program of education and referrals for jobs and training. Director Natalia Davis is currently working with the U.S. Department of Labor to recruit young adults for group classes and placement in jobs.

For Further Information

Any librarian working with young people should know where to turn when they have questions that need answers: Write or call the Executive Director of the Young Adult Services Divi-sion of the American Library Association, 50 East Huron Street, Chicago, IL 60611; telephone 312-944-6780. This office has the finest reputation within our professional association and deserves the membership support of all those who work with young adults. An additional resource at the American Library Association is the Executive Director of the Office of Library Outreach Services; this office acts as liaison and clear-inghouse for much of the library work carried out in ethnic minority communities.

4
Youth Participation in Library Decision Making

JANA VARLEJS

The current surge of interest in youth participation in library planning and policymaking does not reflect the emergence of a brand-new idea in young adult services—responsible youth involvement in library-based activities has been around for a long time. However, it does reflect increased attentiveness and response to the desire of young adults to play effective roles in and through libraries.

A major catalyst for this new interest was the 1979 White House Conference on Library and Information Service (WHCLIS), which produced as one of its 64 resolutions:

BE IT RESOLVED that there be at least one youth appointee named to the National Commission on Libraries and Information Science as a voting member, that States be encouraged to include youths on their library boards as voting members, and that local governments be encouraged to include at least one youth as a voting member on the local library board.

Presented by a youth caucus to the delegates at the conference, the resolution clearly expresses the wish of young people to have much more input in library policy setting and planning than is generally afforded. The ease with which this resolution passed must be attributed, at least in part, to the fact that a significant number of young adults participated in WHCLIS and in the governors' conferences preceding it: Six percent (or 27) of the WHCLIS lay delegates were under age twenty.[1] The question is: What is the most effective way for youth to be heard? The framers of the WHCLIS "youth representation" resolution perceived a seat on policymaking bodies and a vote as the clearest manifestations of the right of youth to take part in the decision-making process. Practically speaking, however, this appears to be impossible to implement. Appointments to commissions or boards not only encounter legal and political obstacles but also do not guarantee any real power to effect change.

Fortunately, young adult participation in library planning and policymaking can be achieved in other ways. Examples of young adult involvement in materials selection, program planning and implementation, public relations, space design, and even policy setting exist. Many of these youth participation models antedate WHCLIS, and all are basically a part of traditional young adult services.

Definition of Terms

Before considering some of the arguments for and against youth participation projects, it is important to clarify the term "youth participation." As it has been defined by the Youth Participation in Library Decision-Making Committee of the American Library Association's Young Adult Services Division (ALA/YASD):

Youth participation in libraries is involvement of young adults in responsible action and significant decision making which affects the design and delivery of library and information services for their peers and the community.[2]

The National Commission on Resources for Youth (NCRY), an organization devoted to expanding opportunities for young people to participate in society, bases its definition upon its own work and experience:

Youth participation is the involving of youth in responsible, challenging action that meets genuine needs, with opportunities for planning and/or decision making affecting others in an activity whose impact or consequence is extended to others—i.e., outside or beyond the youth participants themselves. Other desirable features of youth participation are provisions for critical reflection on the participatory activity and the opportunity for group effort toward a common goal.[3]

Both the YASD and NCRY definitions call for something beyond what librarians generally have asked of YA advisory boards or have given to their members in return. The aim is to give youth a chance to plan and direct activities that have an impact on others and, in the process, to learn from the experience.

In Support of Youth Participation

Experts on adolescent development point out the importance of learning to make choices and decisions, and declare that adolescents must have "practical learning opportunities" and "have a genuine chance to participate as citizens, as members of a household, as workers—in general, as responsible members of society."[4] Libraries can be one of the institutions that gives them that chance.

From the point of view of young adults, the public library is one of the few institutions in the community that is open to and serves all age groups. It does not charge fees, does not mandate attendance, does not give tests or grades. It leaves the young person alone to pursue her or his own devices, unless those are disruptive to the other users of the library. With the exception of the ubiquitous shopping mall, there are not too many places for a teenager to go in most communities. Even for young adults who are heavily involved in sports, creative arts, religious organizations, and other scheduled activities, the public library can be important, simply because it is *not* scheduled. Because the involvement is voluntary, not subject to the reward-rebuke system, and not necessarily confined to the peer group established in the school setting, participation in library decision making can give young adults a taste of the dynamic process that shapes communities, as well as practice in dealing with diverse people, structures, and processes.

From the point of view of young adult librarians, input from the user group helps them to keep up to date with mercurial YA interests, to create effective promotion and new ways of reaching nonusers, and to document the needs of the user group for budgeting and planning purposes. From the point of view of the administrator and trustees, youth involvement has the potential of preparing a cadre of informed and committed library supporters who will soon be taxpayers with real power. In the meantime, young adults can continue to remind parents of the educational and social value of the public library.

In Opposition to Youth Participation

Some question the appropriateness of librarians concerning themselves with the kinds of objectives that the NCRY sees as paramount. They argue that librarians are not trained to be youth counselors, although that role is often thrust upon them. Librarians may also be reluctant to give young adults the kind of power and self-determination essential to true youth participation, particularly when they are working in hierarchical institutions with fairly rigid rules and lines of authority. To give young adults the impression that they can effect change or influence policy when such outcomes are highly unlikely is considered by some to be irresponsible and counterproductive. Yet another argument against applying the NCRY concept of youth participation to the library setting might be the danger of losing sight of the most universally accepted goal of library services for youth, that is, the promotion of reading and learning. Arguments could also be made on the basis of staff and financial resource shortages—youth participation demands a great deal of the librarian's time.

Participation in School Libraries

Although the school library offers a narrower context for decision making, there are still many opportunities for students, librarians, and school administrators to work together. For example, at the state government level, the Illinois State Board of Education has established a Student Advisory Council, one of whose members serves on the board's Library and Media Advisory Council. At the local level, student boards or committees can be effective in providing input for selection and other media center policy: At the D. C. Everest Senior High

School, in Schofield, Wisconsin, students participated in developing a new instructional materials selection and reconsideration policy and will continue to serve on the Reconsideration Committee with equal voting rights.

Northview High School, in Grand Rapids, Michigan, has a media center advisory committee, which is a standing committee within the student government structure. It is composed of one representative for each grade and meets with the director of the media center monthly. Richard Wiltse, media director, reports that he has "gained a better awareness of student attitudes and concerns," and that "the students are also gaining a new awareness of our concerns." The statement of purpose for the group calls for the committee to "establish effective channels of communication between students and the media center staff to work towards achieving the best possible operation to service the needs of all Northview High School students." The duties of the committee are the following:

1. To establish and maintain channels for student input into media center operations and policies
2. To establish and maintain channels for student evaluation of media center services
3. To provide for establishing of special funding, if necessary
4. To provide for student input and assistance in special programs and services the media center may establish
5. To assist in setting priorities and planning of long- and short-range goals
6. To assist in other functions as the need arises

Participation in Public Libraries

Examples of public library projects include a considerable number of advisory boards or councils, few of which, however, deal with overall, rather than strictly youth-related, library matters. One of the rare exceptions is the annual appointment of a student as an ex officio member of the Bergenfield (New Jersey) Public Library board of trustees. The practice was initiated in 1977, when the board was seeking a way to improve ties with the schools and to promote public library use among young adults. The superintendent of schools, who holds a seat on the board, suggested the appointment of a high school student each year in order to facilitate communication. The recommendation was accepted, and a student has sat on the board ever since. Because the superintendent is careful to select a young person who is considered to be a leader and is respected by the student body, the liaison has been fairly effective and has maintained credibility with young adults. All board documents go to the student representative, who participates fully in all discussions. Over the years, the student representative has helped to increase the library's visibility, has generated program ideas, and has communicated young adult needs to the board and to the library administration.

The Spokane (Washington) Public Library has a young adult member on its Community Planning Committee, which is developing a five-year plan as part of the library's planning process. Sixteen-year-old Ken Richards, one of the five members of the committee, has the same responsibilities and voting power as the other members. Ken, who is on the library's Young Adult Advisory Committee, acts as a liaison for the YA community and ensures that their interests are reflected in the plan. He has been an effective member of the group and has gained self-confidence and skill through his participation on the citizen committee.

The Mesa (Arizona) Public Library's Young Adult Advisory Committee selects one of its members to represent it at board of trustees meetings. Unfortunately, this kind of young adult representation is rare.

Participation in YA Services

The picture is brighter in YA services. There are YA advisory groups and YA-controlled programs, publications, and other activities. Young adults have helped to plan and design YA areas in libraries; worked on producing videotapes for library promotion; created and presented programs for children; run book sales and comics swaps; tutored children in reading and math; and participated in radio talk shows. The kinds of involvement that occur vary with the needs identified in a given community and the interests of the young adults.

Advisory boards/councils

As a rule, the starting point is the recruitment of a group of young adults who are already library users and readers, to act in an advisory capacity to librarians on materials selection or program planning. Occasionally, individual teens will ask the librarian informally to program specific activities, such as performance groups, Dungeons and Dragons tournaments, or chess clubs. But, because the typical takeoff point for YA involvement is the youth board or young adult advisory council, and because there is enough information about actual experience with this approach to warrant some generalization, much of what follows will refer to this model.

The librarian's purpose in setting up a council or board is usually related to the promotion of reading. Getting young adults involved in reviewing materials and in programs is seen as a means of increasing library use and stimulating interest in books. Just as important is the desire of the librarian to check her or his judgment in selection against that of representatives of the target group. YA collection budgets are never generous, and one does not want to spend scarce dollars on material that will not be used.

Most young adult librarians know that standards of collection development are not the same for young adults as they are for children. A book that is acclaimed by adult critics may be impossible to "sell" to young adults whose interests do not extend to the theme or setting of the book. On the other hand, a mediocre book on a topic that is currently "in" will find its audience with no promotional effort. The same principle applies to programming—if the topic is not in vogue, the best of programs will fail. As Joan Abrams points out in "No Fail YA Programming," the trick is to identify a "cresting fad."[5] A youth board or advisory council may not guarantee a direct line to this kind of information, but it is bound to help one keep a finger on the rapid pulse of ever-changing teen enthusiasms.

When the YASD Youth Participation in Library Decision-Making Committee sent out brief forms to gather information about youth participation projects, one of the headings was "Purpose of the Project." The following are typical responses:

1. To stimulate reading and interest and awareness of library services
2. To review and evaluate new books
3. To solicit YA input for library programs, services, and book purchases
4. To plan projects and programs suited to the interests of young adults, to help young adults make fuller use of

library services, and to enlist their help in improving those services

5. To get young adults involved in the selection of materials for their peers and to create programs designed to attract other teenagers to the library
6. To provide input from young adults, assist in planning
7. To advise the book selection committee as to what books teens will like and why; also to help the YA librarian bring their views to the YASD Best Books Committee
8. To assist with the total library program
9. To create a department for young adults with materials purchased specifically for them in order to increase YA usage of the library
10. To involve young adults in promoting library materials and in planning programs

Each of these statements of purpose reflects a desire on the part of the librarian to create a mutually beneficial link between the library and the YA community, an awareness of the need to tailor service to user needs, and a rudimentary marketing strategy. Implicit in these statements is the goal of providing library materials and services that are responsive to YA interests and that will be used.

The commonality found in the statements of purpose is also evident in the descriptions of the projects. In the majority of responses, librarians indicated that they meet every two weeks or monthly with the YA group to review and discuss new books (and sometimes films), work on a publication, and plan programs. Although special events or projects are not unusual, activity tends to focus on library materials selection and promotion and program planning and publicity.

Some libraries, however, are giving young adults a measure of control over rules governing the use of the YA area and collection. At the Northborough (Massachusetts) Free Library, an advisory committee was recruited to participate in the planning and implementation of a new YA room specifically for the middle school group. The committee members not only helped in selecting materials, decorating the room, and organizing the opening celebration but they also decided on circulation policies. When younger children began to use the room, the advisory group was asked to recommend a policy. They decided that the younger children should be allowed when accompanied by a middle schooler—a brother or sister, a friend, or a baby-sitter—but that high school students should not be allowed to stay, "because they are likely to intimidate the kids the room was meant for." According to the project director, from the outset objectives included setting reasonable rules and regulations for the use of the room and evaluating the project on a continuing basis.

The Elkhart Public Library Young Friends group was initiated with the following goals in mind:

Aims
1. To improve library services for young adults in the community.
2. To help young adults make fuller use of the services and opportunities the library offers.

Benefits to Members
1. It is an opportunity to learn how to conduct meetings, to work on committees, to plan successful programs, and to learn leadership skills.
2. It is an opportunity to learn how a public library functions and what library resources are invaluable to you in college and on the job.
3. It is an opportunity to learn more about your community and to contribute to its cultural enrichment.
4. It is an opportunity to meet new people, to be brought into contact with new ideas, to express your own ideas and see results, and to develop communication skills useful in college and on the job.

This is one of the few projects that states explicitly that leadership and citizenship skills development is part of the purpose of youth involvement.

Even "Levels," the model library-based youth participation project, at Great Neck (New York) Library, does not spell out its role of nurturing decision-making skills, although its organization and administration cannot help but do so. A remarkable amount of self-determination is encouraged, with youth participation not only in planning but also in hiring staff, peer discipline, and routine policy determination. The major purpose of Levels, however, is to provide a place for constructive activities for young people, and this purpose has been amply met since the inception of the center in 1974. As described in Levels introductory brochure, the range of activities is wide and diverse:

Some classes like guitar, drama, drawing and dance have been continuous; others, like our "relationships" group or our S.A.T. prep course, have run for shorter periods. We've also presented all kinds of musical concerts—from rock and disco to jazz and classical—and staged over 35 major and minor theatrical productions like "Hair," "Man of La Mancha," "Jesus Christ Superstar" and "West Side Story" as well as mixed media and original dramas.

We have film fests, poetry readings, coffee houses, international nights, dances, photography exhibits, softball, barbecues, spontaneous happenings and lots of other things.

Not every library has the space or the funds for staff to emulate Levels, but the principles of self-rule, appropriate personnel, and a responsive environment can surely be adopted by any library.

Cooperation with other agencies

Although the advisory board is by far the predominant means of involving young adults in decision making, some variations on the model can be found. For example, libraries may cooperate with other agencies in fostering youth participation. The Woodbridge (New Jersey) Public Library sponsors a Mayor's Youth Committee, which has the support of the town council, as well as the mayor and the library administration. The committee's purpose is "to involve youth in the decision making process with respect to the library and the township [and] to address the concerns of youth within the township . . . [such as] employment, transportation, activities for youth, and community involvement." Because this is, perhaps, a unique library-related youth project, a summary of its activities follows:

1. Annual summer rock concerts—six weekly concerts held in July and August. The bands are local groups, usually willing to perform for free, recruited through press releases and radio spots (also word of mouth).

2. A walk-a-thon to raise funds for cystic fibrosis. (CF is the number one genetic killer of young people.) The walk-a-

thon is open to all ages and family involvement is encouraged.

3. A job bank list of businesses in the township willing to hire teenagers is in the information gathering stage. When completed it will be distributed to all library agencies and school guidance counselors.

4. Senior citizen/youth friendly visiting program—teenage volunteers and senior citizens who are somewhat isolated socially are linked together. Cosponsored by Woodbridge Multiservices to the Aging.

5. Plans for a job fair are in the discussion stages.

6. Young adult librarians constantly interview their YA patrons as to their program ideas and materials needs. The committee also reacts to these areas.

In Baltimore, an unusual cooperative youth participation project involves Enoch Pratt Free Library and the Family Circle Theatre, Inc., of the Baltimore Council on Adolescent Pregnancy, Parenting, and Pregnancy Prevention. The library contributes performance space in its branches and publicity for the troupe of teen players, who present improvisational skits dealing with issues of human growth and sexuality. Enoch Pratt's Linda Lapides reports that:

Teenage actors and actresses seek to involve their audiences in discussion after the open-ended vignettes. It is felt that since teenagers are so effective in influencing other teenagers this was the best way to reach and influence a usually hard-to-reach age group. The audience is not limited to teenagers. In fact, a mixture of adults and teens often produces a better question-and-answer session than an audience composed solely of adolescents. The student actors and actresses literally hold the audiences in the palm of their hand. They are responsible for the content of the dramas and for leading the discussion afterward. . . . The drawback is that there is some concern that the values that the group is attempting to highlight do not clearly come through.[6]

This project does not fit the YASD definition for youth participation in library decision making, but it certainly does fit the more general NCRY definition. Cooperation with agencies such as the Baltimore Council and the Woodbridge Multiservices to the Aging agency in efforts to involve youth in educational or cultural activities is a good way for libraries to expand service programs while gaining experience with youth participation.

Single-purpose activities

Some library-based youth participation projects are single-purpose activities designed to meet a specific need or interest. Youth tutoring youth, making a videotape, and storytelling or puppeteer performances for younger children are examples of activities that meet many of the criteria of youth participation, although they may not affect library policy.

Implementing a Program

It is important to realize that there are benefits to be gained from any youth participation project, but that the benefits to the young participants and to the library will vary in nature and in proportion. The library may invest a great deal of staff time in working with a small group of young adults who reap enormous rewards in personal growth, learning, and enjoyment—a book discussion group or poetry workshop are examples. On the other hand, a smaller amount of time spent in soliciting reader feedback or purchase suggestions can greatly aid the librarian without doing much for the young adults beyond making them feel that their opinions count. Both activities are worthwhile and have their place, but a decision on which route to take should be made only after the librarian has thought through all the options, established priorities in terms of both YA and library needs, and assessed the cost benefits of those alternatives that promise to meet priority needs.

Ideally, the library should provide for two levels of YA participation. The first level would involve a small number of young adults in planning and setting policy and such responsibilities as directing programs and editing publications. At the second level, many more young adults would be taking part in such activities as tutoring, visiting the homebound, writing reviews and other items for a publication, and presenting programs for children such as story hours. At each level, the librarian must remember the dual purpose of youth participation in libraries: to improve library service for young adults and to provide young adults with opportunities to learn and exercise leadership skills in a community institution setting. Guidelines prepared by the YASD Youth Participation in Library Decision-Making Committee, reproduced in Appendix I of this book, can help the librarian to plan carefully and to anticipate potential problems.

A successful program

In implementing youth participation, the most important requirement is genuine commitment on the part of the library's governing body, administration, and staff. All must believe that young adults have a positive contribution to make and must be willing to act upon reasonable recommendations made by the youth group. In addition, the library must make the investment in staff time needed to train, guide, and support the group in its efforts. The young adult librarian, or whoever acts as the adult facilitator, must be a person who interacts well with youth, is skilled in group dynamics, and can guide rather than dominate or manipulate. As one young person put it, the adult facilitator should be one "who can direct students into positive action; give information about alternatives and help students solve their problems, not solve them for them."[7] Enthusiasm, a sense of humor, and patience are also very helpful.

Given full administrative support and a good facilitator, the next requirement is a core group of young adults who have an interest in the library and are willing to devote some time on a regular basis. Some public librarians have been successful in recruiting through the schools, by consulting with teachers and school librarians, or by calling for volunteers directly through visiting school clubs or classes. The advantage of recruiting through schools is the greater likelihood of ending up with a group that is made up of people from different schools and backgrounds and that is therefore, more representative of the community as a whole. Others prefer to invite regular library users on an individual basis: The Northland Public Library in Pittsburgh draws its YA advisory committee from its complement of teen pages. The Tampa-Hillsborough County Public Library System and the Spokane Public Library use fliers distributed in the library and through the schools to both recruit young adults and solicit ideas. Once a few people are involved, they often bring friends.

Local radio stations, posters in places where the young congregate, and stories in newspapers that have youth sections should not be neglected. Even when the use of mass media channels fails to enlist volunteers, it sends the message to the community at large that the library wants to involve young people in its programs and values the contribution that they can make to a community institution. We should never forget the enormous response generated by John F. Kennedy's invocation, "Ask not what your country can do for you, but what you can do for your country!"

A number of librarians advise that one should start small and limit initial efforts to a single-purpose project that will generate a product, such as a newsletter featuring book reviews. An example is *The New YARC Times* of the Charles County (Maryland) Bryans Road Branch Library, which has attracted members to the group and is now only one of a number of projects sponsored by the Young Adult Reading Club (YARC). The YA group at the Leominster (Massachusetts) Public Library also produces a newsletter, which includes artwork, poetry, jokes, and program announcements. YA librarian Diane Sanabria reports that "The newsletter staff is our 'nucleus,' . . . and many of the teens who have become involved, active members were friends of original teen staff members." The younger the group, the more important the doing, as opposed to the discussing. Jean Langley of the Northborough Free Library reports that her sixth- to eighth-grade group had the most fun on the days that they actually helped to refurbish the room that was to be theirs and on the day of the opening party.

On the subject of parties and other social activity, YA librarians agree: They are very important! Initially, they help "break the ice," and later they are the best way for the library to show its appreciation to the young people who have contributed time, energy, and imagination to making the library a more dynamic and responsive place. As with any volunteer activity, recognition and rewards are vital to continuing success. More important, fun and excitement as regular ingredients of YA participation will do more to ensure its survival than any amount of recruiting.

Another important factor is the training and orientation given to the young adults. Unfortunately, there is almost no information on how librarians handle this. The very lack of information suggests that it is done on an as-you-go basis, but further study of effective projects should be done. The experience of NCRY strongly points to the need for carefully planned methods to help youth acquire group decision-making skills, as well as those needed for the specific activity chosen by the group. For example, young adults who undertake storytelling for young children or visiting nursing homes for the elderly need to know what to expect, how to deal with problems, what will interest the people they will be meeting, and what will make them feel comfortable with each other. NCRY also makes the point that it is essential for young adults to discuss what happened afterward, so that they may have the chance to analyze problems and successes. It is this kind of "debriefing" that fosters learning and development, helping a young person to derive general insights from specific experiences and to modify behavior in light of these insights. This process of analysis need not be intimidating to the YA librarian. It is enough for the adult facilitator to create the occasion for discussion; she or he is not required to be a trained counselor. Given a receptive environment and motivation for reflection, young adults will usually learn what they need to learn.

There are several good sources listed in the bibliography that will give the reader further guidance on implementing a youth participation project. The forthcoming *Youth Participation in Libraries* from NCRY and YASD includes case studies as well as guidelines. Evie Wilson's two articles on youth advisory boards are filled with practical advice based on experience.

The unanswered questions

A library model for youth participation is indeed beginning to emerge, but it must be recognized that the concept of youth participation in library decision making is just beginning to be explored in all its ramifications, and no one has the answers to all the questions that might arise. For example:

1. What is the best way to assess the effectiveness of youth participation in library decision making?
2. What training do librarians need in order to help them be good youth participation facilitators?
3. How are young adults best trained in skills they need for participation and decision making?
4. What kinds of policies should be developed to ensure that responsibilities and degree of autonomy of youth are clear to both young adults and library officials?

5. What is the best way to give youth a real voice in the governance of the library as a whole, not just its services for young adults?

6. How does one guard against tokenism and exploitation of young adults?

More experience with youth involvement in library planning and policy setting is needed before questions such as these can be answered. It is disappointing that there are so few models of successful YA participation today, more than thirty years after youth councils were first recommended by the American Library Association.[8] Both the 1960 and 1977 ALA publications on services for young adults also stipulated that young adults should be involved in planning and other participatory and consultative roles.[9] The many barriers to youth participation must be overcome, however, if the library is to provide vital and responsive service for a major segment of the community and to gain the allegiance and support of its future adults.

In Retrospect

As the WHCLIS experience has shown, young people care very much about libraries and can be highly effective champions of the right to read. In reporting on the New York Governor's Conference, *American Libraries* said, ". . . the show stealer was 12-year-old delegate David Abraham of Youngstown, who defended freedom of access for young people with astonishing wit, poise, and forcefulness . . . his contribution in Albany was second to none."[10]

Four years later, when David Abraham responded to the YASD survey of WHCLIS youth representatives, he said, ". . . memories of adults who seriously considered limiting access to libraries by young people still rankle with me. When adults accept youth as *reading* partners and help them to develop a love of reading, co-decision making will simply become a more efficient way of doing things."

Jennifer Casolo, who was seventeen when she was a delegate to the Connecticut Governor's Conference in 1978, wrote the following in 1982: "Libraries should not only hold and offer the information most needed in the community, but should offer information and programs to improve the community. To *in-*

form is not passive and is not to react. *Activity* is what is missing in too many libraries. . . . I'd like to see libraries as an active part of our educational systems."

There are David Abrahams and Jennifer Casolos throughout the country. To ignore them and to fail to offer them an opportunity to take an active role in making the library an educational and cultural force in the community is wasteful, foolish, and shortsighted.

Notes

1. *Information for the 1980's: Final Report of the White House Conference on Library and Information Services, 1979* (Washington, D.C.: U.S. Government Printing Office, 1980), p. 739.

2. "Guidelines for Youth Participation in Library Decision Making," prepared by the Youth Participation in Library Decision-Making Committee, Young Adult Services Division, American Library Association, as a handout for the YASD President's Program on Youth Participation, July 1982. Much of the information presented in this chapter is based on the work of this committee.

3. *An Introductory Manual on Youth Participation for Program Administrators*, prepared by National Commission on Resources for Youth (Washington, D.C.: Department of Health, Education, and Welfare, Office of Youth Development, Division of Youth Activities, 1976), p. 4.

4. Gisela Konopka, "Requirements for Healthy Development of Adolescent Youth," *Adolescence* 8 (Fall 1973): 303 ff.

5. Joan Abrams, "No Fail YA Programming," *Voice of Youth Advocates* 5 (October 1982): 19–20, 24.

6. Correspondence to the Youth Participation in Library Decision-Making Committee, Young Adult Services Division, American Library Association.

7. "Students' Perceptions of the Good Adult Facilitator," *Resources for Youth* 9 (Spring 1980): 1.

8. *The Public Library Plans for the Teen Age*, prepared by the Committee on Post-War Planning, American Library Association, Division of Libraries for Children and Young People and Its Section, the Young People's Reading Round Table (Chicago: American Library Association, 1948), p. 6.

9. *Young Adult Services in the Public Library*, prepared by the Committee on Standards for Work with Young Adults in Public Libraries, Public Library Association, American Library Association (Chicago: American Library Association, 1960); and *Directions for Library Services to Young Adults*, Services Statement Development Committee, Young Adult Services Division, American Library Association (Chicago: American Library Association, 1977). References to seeking young adult input and involvement are scattered throughout both publications.

10. Art Plotnik, "The Library Liberals Say 'Yes' at New York's White House Preconference," *American Libraries* 9 (September 1978): 452.

Bibliography

Directions for Library Service to Young Adults. Services Statement Development Committee, Young Adult Services Division, American Library Association. Chicago, 1977.

An Introductory Manual on Youth Participation for Program Administrators. National Commission on Resources for Youth. Washington, D.C.: Department of Health, Education, and Welfare, Office of Youth Development, Division of Youth Activities, 1976.

Konopka, Gisela. "Requirements for Healthy Development of Adolescent Youth." *Adolescence* 8 (Fall 1973): 291–315.

Maminsky, Dolores. "Youth Helping Youth." *Voice of Youth Advocates* 5 (December 1982): 18–20.

Wilson, Evie. "The Young Adult Advisory Board: Decision Making as Recreation and Responsibility." *The Bookmark* 37 (Winter 1978): 55–59.

———. "The Young Adult Advisory Board: How to Make It Work." *Voice of Youth Advocates* 2 (April 1979): 11–14.

Youth Participation in School and Public Libraries. National Commission on Resources for Youth with the Young Adult Services Division, American Library Association. Boston: National Commission on Resources for Youth, 1983. Jointly distributed by NCRY and ALA/YASD.

5
Merchandising Collections and Services

ELLEN V. LIBRETTO

Training in merchandising techniques develops a natural and essential skill for all staff, but is of particular importance to the young adult librarian. The appeal of merchandising is to all age levels, but especially to teenagers who respond to the commercialism of the bookstore look; it is through effective and attractive merchandising of the public library collection that the young adult librarian can shine.

Merchandising projects in libraries can take on varying forms, depending on the immediate goals of the project, the funds available for purchase of books and display-type furniture, and the attitude of management and staff toward the project. From the point of embarkation on the project, the library administration must not only be united in its efforts to support the staff's early efforts at marketing but must also be willing to examine past and current practices of collection development, book selection, and patterns of purchase and to help remove impediments to the implementation of merchandising techniques.

The focus of this article is Queens Borough Public Library, a large urban public library system in New York City that implemented bookstore merchandising techniques in its sixty branches, resulting in a 16 percent circulation increase system-wide in the first year of the project. In the second year of the merchandising experiment (fiscal year 1982–1983), the projected circulation is 8.3 million, which represents a 43 percent increase in circulation since the merchandising project began in the summer of 1981. The staff training project, which proved to be a constructive and energizing force for unifying management and staff intent on producing changes in collection needs and staff attitudes, can be adapted for in-service workshops at the system, regional, or statewide level.

B. Dalton Comes to Queens

In 1981, the Queens Borough Public Library decided to work toward increasing circulation in its ten branch libraries with the lowest circulations. This decision led the management of the library to rethink some of the current methods of book purchase and collection development and also allowed for the revamping and revitalization of collections. The staff began to look for new ways to project materials to make the libraries more appealing to current users and to nonusers as well.

For several years, the staff had used such tried and true outreach service techniques as visits to school classes, work with senior citizens, and film and theater performances; indeed, the entire gamut of enhanced services had been tried in an earnest effort to become more responsive to specific community needs, to bring in new users, and to give better services to the staple library patron. Some small circulation increases did occur from time to time in the ten low-circulation units, but, overall, circulation was not maintained and would even fall, in spite of the aggressive outreach programs.

The first seeds of merchandising were planted by the deputy director in summer 1981, when $50,000 was allocated to the ten low-circulation branches for the purchase of popular reading and survival skills paperbacks for children, teenagers, and adults. In addition, large numbers of bookstore wire racks were purchased to display the books face-out. Titles were ordered in multiples to ease the problems of arrangement that library staff experience during a shift in collection emphasis from hardcover to paperback.

To test the appeal of bookstore merchandising in the library, the young adult consultant introduced several publisher's dumps (the cardboard book-display units seen in bookstores), mainly Sweet Dreams (Bantam) and Silhouette Young Love (Simon & Schuster). The reaction from libraries that had purchased the dumps with multiple copies of the numbered titles was immediate and positive. Across the board, branches reported that teenagers were taking out stacks of material from the dumps and that, by midafternoon, the dump stock was depleted and had to be replenished with like material. The success of the dumps encouraged the library to proceed with its merchandising plans.

While the branches were shifting collection emphasis to paperbacks, the library administration called in a marketing specialist from B. Dalton to share with the staff some of the fine points that booksellers have developed to merchandise paperbacks. A systemwide meeting attended by representatives from each library was held in a branch selected because it represented features common to more than half of the branches. In planning sessions with the B. Dalton representative, the library administration stressed the need to get the most mileage out of physical plants, budgets, and staff in a period of limited resources, in order to meet the needs of a public also constrained by a tight economy.

The B. Dalton training session took a twofold approach. First, because the workshop was conducted by a nonlibrarian representing a major corporation with a proven track record for success, it was established early on that matching books and people was the common goal for both the librarian and bookstore owner. Second were the practical suggestions: improvement of paperback book arrangement through better use of floor space; subject categorization of material; face-out shelving; impulse circulations (placing small groups of titles with surefire appeal—with catchy titles for mysteries, science fiction, and love stories—on top of catalogs, tables, circulation desks, and in other eye-catching places in the library); and the use of floor and tabletop dumps with headers to identify quickly the titles or subject.

The library had already experimented with dumps in the ten low-circulation branches and had discovered that dumps convey an impression of abundance to the reader, who is enticed by availability of multiple copies of titles, with easy access to the author's previous titles or similar titles by others. The headers also attract readers, and the compact arrangement of titles encourages impulse circulation.

Merchandising Guidelines

The following guidelines for merchandising techniques in public libraries were developed by the Merchandising Committee of the Queens Borough Public Library. These guidelines present the ways and means for agencies to better promote their collections and services to users. They are flexible enough so that every agency and division can be guided by them. They do not preclude individual creativity and resourcefulness, but encourage it. The effective use of merchandising and display techniques requires practice and experimentation.

I. *Means and Methods*
   A. Shelving
     1. Conventional
       a. Displaying titles face-out at ends of shelves and atop shelves
       b. Where possible, lowering rear shelf brackets one notch and slanting shelves down
         (1) Titles with multiple copies can be shelved with alternate spine-out and face-out
     2. Special display shelving
       a. Well suited to merchandising because slanted
       b. Titles can be shelved spine-out and face-out
     3. Paperback racks
       a. Face-out
   B. Displays
     1. Library windows and display cases
     2. Tables—well suited to temporary, small, special-interest, and current displays
     3. Book troughs
     4. Bulletin boards
     5. Pyramids/step displays
       a. Can be created by stacking boxes into pyramid or step shape
       b. Can be created with books alone
       c. Can be built anywhere—floor, counter, table
       d. Most useful for thematic or subject displays—easier to replenish
       e. Well suited for multiple copies

(1) Books should be placed flat on their back covers with spine visible

(2) Additional copy or copies of a book should be placed on top of the pile with the cover face-out in the direction of a patron's line of vision

   f. Should be well stocked at all times

6. Dumps
   a. Versatile and effective for display
   b. Ideally a paperback dump should contain one title; three is the maximum number for a nine-section dump
   c. If more than one title is used in a dump, arrange the copies face-out in vertical columns
   d. May be used for thematic displays
   e. Small dumps can be effectively used on tables and counters
   f. Should be located head-on or at no more than a 45 degree angle to the patron's line of vision
   g. Paperbacks in a dump should never face spine-out

7. Other display equipment
   a. Special racks, e.g., Sunset publications
   b. Slanted magazine shelving can be used for many different kinds of library materials
   c. Book trucks—can be used as temporary display areas in conjunction with current programs, assignments, etc.
   d. Floor—multiple copies in stacks or pyramids

C. Signs
   1. Should be simple
   2. Should be colorful—primary colors are more eye-catching than secondary
   3. Should be plentiful
      a. Wherever there are displays
      b. Branches should have on hand a supply with standard headings and captions

D. Inserts
   1. To be placed directly in books on display
   2. Should entice reader to borrow the book

II. *Branch Modifications for Merchandising*
   A. Rearrangement of stacks, furniture, etc., where possible, to create browsing areas
   B. Relocation of collections to provide optimum exposure and use
   C. Relocation of service areas for better organization and use

III. *Display Locations/Positioning*
   Assess normal traffic flow, determine locations that are readily accessible to patron, and locate displays in those areas.

III. *Display Locations/Positioning (cont'd)*
  A. Up front
    1. Entrance is the most trafficked area with well-defined pathways
    2. Best suited for concentration of eye-appealing, well-chosen, and well-stocked displays
    3. Prime area for new books, dumps, etc.
  B. Ends of cross-aisles
    1. Also heavy traffic areas
    2. Displays at ends of cross-aisles will easily be seen by great number of people
    3. Good location for dumps
  C. Eye level
    1. Concentrate materials on shelves generally located between 36 inches and 60 inches
    2. Put fewer items on shelves above and below so that borrower can scan more easily
  D. Circulation desk area
    1. Ideal location for "impulse borrowing"
    2. Suitable items for the area
      a. Topical material, movie or television tie-ins, news
      b. Holiday or seasonal material
      c. Library program tie-in material
  E. Open floor
    1. Displays on tabletops
    2. Dumps
  F. At an angle to patron traffic
    1. Displays such as dumps should be directed ahead of and facing patron's line of vision or at an angle of 45 degrees or less along the same line

IV. *What to Merchandise*
  A. New and popular titles
    1. Hardcover
    2. Paperback
    3. Seven-day and pay collection
  B. Fiction
    1. Good old titles
    2. Classics
      a. Standard—Dickens, Twain, etc.
      b. Modern—Fitzgerald, Plath, etc.
    3. Designated authors and/or genre, e.g., gothics
    4. Titles on television, in the movies, and on Broadway
  C. Nonfiction
    1. Subjects of popular interest
    2. New specialized titles
    3. Subjects of current interest—world events, Reaganomics, etc.

4. Biographies—old and new, historical and contemporary
D. Paperbacks
  1. Mass market—fiction and nonfiction
  2. Trade—fiction and nonfiction
  3. Multiple copies of titles for student use, particularly when special assignments are known, e.g., Shakespeare, plays, classics; these titles should be shelved separately
  4. Preparation and shelving
    a. Preparation of paperbacks should be minimal using no cards, pockets, or labels for the author's name
    b. Mystery, western, science fiction, and romance labels are permissible
    c. The tops of the books can be coded in *pencil* only (magic marker ink smears) for subject and/or classification designation
E. Pamphlets
  1. New acquisitions
  2. Special-interest topics—drug abuse, abortion, etc.
F. Magazines and newspapers
  1. New acquisitions
  2. Circulating titles
    a. Shelve with regular collection according to subject, i.e., sports, interior decorating, cooking, etc.
    b. Should be used along with books and paperbacks for topical and subject displays
G. Records and cassettes
H. Subjects of community interest
  1. Education
  2. Jobs
  3. Consumerism
  4. Local history
  5. Local government and agencies

V. *Who Merchandises*
  A. Librarians
    1. Responsible for overall merchandising in agency
    2. Purchase materials according to merchandising goals, i.e., in subject areas and quantity according to demand—current and anticipated
    3. Plan merchandising areas with regard to traffic patterns, visibility, and accessibility
    4. Establish subject categories, coding, and locator markings for hardcover and paperback items to be merchandised
    5. Designate specific areas, shelves, and displays to pages and clerks for merchandising
    6. Ensure that sufficient copies, titles, records, cassettes, etc., are available for replenishing circulated copies
    7. Request needed signs and headers for racks, areas, etc.

V. *Who Merchandises (cont'd)*
  B. Clerks
    1. Paperback racks—replenish as copies circulate (replacements should be held on storage shelves in specified workroom area)
    2. New fiction, seven-day, and pay collections—should be put on shelves, troughs, etc., as they are returned, if not needed for reserves
    3. Other areas as instructed by librarian
  C. Pages
    1. Should be instructed how to shelve for merchandising
      a. Special areas, e.g., new and popular
      b. Regular shelves—face-out at ends of shelves and atop stacks
    2. Should be aware of any special and/or locator markings on books for display and merchandising purposes
  D. All staff
    1. Be aware of appearance of merchandised areas—empty spaces, disarray, etc.
    2. Replenish items that circulate on a regular basis, e.g., daily, hourly, etc.
    3. Know where items for restocking areas are stored to ensure quick retrieval
    4. Be aware of slow-moving or unsuccessful displays (clerks and pages should notify librarians who can change or relocate display)

Expanding the Merchandising Concept

The implementation of the merchandising techniques suggested by B. Dalton, combined with trial and error experimentation by the staff, resulted in a 43.3 percent increase in circulation in 1981–1982 over 1980–1981 for the ten branch libraries previously classified as low-circulation units. Taking the cue from the successes of the ten low-circulation units, other branches of the library eagerly began their own merchandising programs, expanding their paperback collections by acquiring dumps, experimenting with various kinds of subject arrangement, and designing headers for particular appeal to community needs. These libraries, too, saw immediate increases in circulation. Frequent regional and systemwide meetings on merchandising results were held so that staff could share successes and avoid common failures.

New guidelines for paperback book purchase were developed by the library administration to remove all impediments to materials acquisition. Branch libraries were encouraged to order directly from the jobber via jobber catalogs and monthly lists, avoiding internal library delays. Shipments were delivered to branches in a few days, with delivery for phone-in orders possible the same day.

It was now time for the library administration to take a look at the current status of the hardcover collections in the branches and to develop guidelines for the merchandising of the bulwark of the system's materials.

A mini-branch experiment

An opportunity to continue to expand and experiment with merchandising techniques on a larger scale, integrating paperbacks with hardcover books, came about when the system's second largest branch, the Flushing Library, was scheduled for closing during a renovation and expansion period. The library administration, not wanting to deprive the borrowers of access to books during the anticipated ten-month renovation period, decided to convert two small basement rooms of the library to a mini-branch, using only display-type furniture, with lighted tops for the insertion of signs to denote the broad subject areas.

It was in the setting up of the Flushing Mini-Library that all the principles of bookstore merchandising came into play. In the greatly reduced space that the two small rooms provided, the library staff had to sift through the basic collection to select approximately 5 percent of the book stock. These basic hardcover books then had to be arranged by broad subject classification such as You and Your Job, Humor, Spanish Books, Classics—old and new, Fiction, and Travel. Approximately $30,000 in paperbacks, on a broad range of subjects, were then added to the display shelving. Books were placed on the shelving in multiples of titles, mixing hardcovers and paperbacks, with alternating spine-out and face-out, always taking maximum advantage of the cover design to catch the eye of the reader.

The temporary quarters of the library opened to the public, with no card catalog, no reference material (although rumor has it that an atlas and a World Book Encyclopedia set were stashed away in the staff room for some ready-reference work), and no chairs and tables. The results were astounding. Not only did circulation rise in dramatic disproportion to the number of books available, but the public responded with a levity and spontaneity associated with a bookstore environment. The most noticeable difference in attitude and usage was from teenagers. Choose Your Own Adventure dumps were sacked, and it also was fortunate for the library that the romance revolution in books for teenagers and adults coincided with its foray into the merchandising arena.

After the facility's renovation was completed, some of the display-type furniture was integrated with traditional library shelving to maintain some of the merchandising look that was so appealing to both the public and the staff in the mini-library. The display units are used to highlight books on some of the most asked for subjects—including job and career information, mysteries, science fiction, and travel. Other sections of the display furniture were recycled for the Queensboro Hill Branch.

A model urban library

The Queensboro Hill Branch, a typical New York City library in terms of size and neighborhood served, opened in June 1982 and functions as a model urban library managed by the principles of merchandising. (See Chapter 14 for an account of the genesis of this library.) Instead of allowing the traditional separate space for children, young adults, and adults (as most public libraries do), this branch has introduced shelving of books on display-type furniture, integrating the collection, and, for the most part, interfiling age-level materials. The children's section here can be identified by a child center, which allows for the shelving of picture books face-out, in tiers. Mothers and grandmothers with children can always be spotted, sitting under the canopy of the child center, on little stools, making major and minor literary discoveries. The young adult nook is punctuated with all of the current dumps stuffed with romances, movie-television tie-ins, as well as tried-and-true paperback titles. Classics and other YA fiction titles are shelved on traditional library shelving with hardcovers and paperbacks displayed in alternate face-out, spine-out arrangement, again always taking full advantage of the attractiveness of the book's cover to catch the eye of the public. Adult fiction and nonfiction are heavily represented in paperback, but a basic branch collection of hardcover titles shelved in display units by subject tends to move in and out at a faster rate than in other branch libraries where books are shelved spine-out by Dewey. In its first six months, the library has exceeded annual projected circulation estimates by 80 percent.

New Challenges for Librarianship

The major responsibility in carrying out the merchandising objectives rests with the online library staffers who day by day watch the public's response to their merchandising techniques. It is the online staffer who tests the barometer of patron response daily, interpreting and serving specific community demands as effectively as possible with the resources at hand. Constant attention to the order and reorder of materials for the ever-changing merchandised collection places pressure on the librarian to order correctly. Although mistakes in ordering unnecessary paperback titles can be rectified in a bookstore when the manager tears off the cover for a return, the librarian is not allowed this luxury. Pioneers in library merchandising soon learn that mistakes are costly and that every book must earn its space on the shelf.

When a library decides to promote the collection in the merchandising style, purchases should be examined with an eye toward their merchandising potential. All other materials held by the library must then also be examined—such as pamphlets, cassettes, records, ready-reference compendiums, videotapes—for the merchandising opportunities that they present. Gaining mastery of the collection, to expand the reading interests of the patron, and to encourage new readers, remains the challenge of the librarian with or without merchandising. But it is especially in working with those patrons who have special needs—the handicapped, the information-poor, and the poor reader—that effective use of merchandising techniques becomes the key to the use of the whole collection.

Early pioneers of merchandising techniques in public libraries have much to learn about the long-range effects of trade practices on the future of the public library. Although instant increases in circulation are indeed gratifying to a public service staff, myriad other factors can also contribute to increased library use—a period of national recession, a commuting public (paperbacks wear well on train and bus rides), decreased budgets for school libraries, increased hours of public service, and shorter loan periods, for example. But using merchandising as a primary showcase for experimentation in collection development does help staff to deal with diminishing resources and to gain the attention of the public. It is the goal of every librarian to continue to expand the reader's access to the greatest range of materials and to allow the public the pleasure of exploring the collection. Implementation and practice of the principles of merchandising can help peak in the librarian the period of the greatest creative energy.

Bibliography

Bronson, Que, and Holly Stone. *Materials Display Manual*. Annapolis, Md.: Public Library of Annapolis and Anne Arundel County, 1981. Covers the entire gamut of displaying materials (books, canned goods, drugstore items). Gives the librarian clues on how to make the most out of displaying library materials.

Green, Sylvie A. "Merchandising Techniques and Libraries." *School Library Journal* 28, no. 1 (September 1981): 35–39. Tips on how the Dallas Public Library entered the merchandising era.

II
Young Adult Literature

6
Writing for Young Adults: An Author's Perspective

GEORGE SULLIVAN

I've been writing nonfiction books for young readers since the mid-1960s, and I have more than a hundred books in print. During the time that I have been writing, I have often heard the juvenile book field, and young adult publishing, in particular, described as being in "a state of flux." Indeed, that has been a stock phrase used through the years to describe conditions.

When I first started having books published, there was much talk about federal government subsidies for book purchases, a subject I hardly hear mentioned any more. Audiovisual aids were coming into vogue, and the trade press was always featuring articles on what impact they might be going to have on book publishing. Paperbacks were being described as the wave of the future. (Of course, they're *always* being described as the wave of the future.) There was a demand for good biography, for science and nature books, for humor and picture books, and just about everyone wanted to do books about blacks.

Because I was quite sports-oriented at the time, much more so than I am now, I decided it would be a good idea to write a biography of the new heavyweight champion of the world, a fresh and exciting young man named Cassius Clay. I was able to coax a contract for the book out of Fleet Press, a small publisher, actually a book-publishing subsidiary of General Features Corporation, a newspaper syndicate for which I was doing a column at the time.

Once the contract was signed, I went to visit Clay (he didn't become Muhammad Ali until a year or so after the book was published) at the Hotel Theresa in Harlem, where he had a suite of rooms. He was lying on his bed, fully dressed, his arms across his chest, and was staring at the ceiling when I met him. Once the introductions were out of the way, I announced that I was about to become his biographer. His expression didn't change. "Nobody's going to write a book about me," he said, "unless I get $50,000." Since that amount was exactly $48,500 more than I was going to receive to write the book, I knew it was going to be difficult for us to come to an agreement.

Anyway, I wrote the book, getting only the barest cooperation from the biographee. His mother, who lived in Louisville, tried to be helpful. But when I went to Louisville to interview her, she kept repeating anecdotes about her son's childhood and upbringing that had already appeared in *Sports Illustrated.* I never made up my mind whether the anecdotes came from her originally, or whether she read them in the magazine and decided to add them to her repertoire.

The anecdotes didn't make any difference. No one wanted to read about Clay—or Ali—and the book sold about nine copies. I've often thought that Fleet simply should have stored the copies in a vault somewhere and started selling them in the 1980s, because the book is now quite valuable among collectors of sports memorabilia.

The Seventies

About the best evidence I have of the many changes that have taken place in young adult book publishing is the books I've written. Those that I'm working on now and those that I've had published in the past year or so are much different from the titles I had published during the 1970s. They're different in style, subject matter, and physical appearance.

For example, I used to write sports biographies for G. P. Putnam's. Bart Starr, a quarterback for the Green Bay Packers, and New York Met pitcher Tom Seaver were two of the several athletes I profiled. These biographies were about 30,000 words, or 160 pages, in length. They were intended for readers age ten and up. They had no illustrations.

School libraries used to buy them. I understand that some teachers used them with so-called reluctant readers. A boy who was a fan of Bart Starr or Tom Seaver would be so eager to learn about his hero that he'd *force* himself to read about him. I guess that was the theory.

All of these books sold well, and some of them sold exceptionally well. The Bart Starr biography went back to press four or five times. (The Putnam accounting department is vague about the exact number.) And I happen to have a copy of one of the very early books in the series, a biography of Lou Gehrig by Frank Graham, a much respected writer of the 1940s and 1950s. "Twenty-sixth printing," the jacket flap says.

Putnam's is no longer publishing books like these. Neither is anyone else. A biography of Roger Staubach, a quarterback for the Dallas Cowboys, was the last book I did in the series. The Staubach book was published in 1974.

The Eighties

Thanks mainly to television, I suppose, young readers no longer want to wade through 160 pages of printed matter, no matter who or what the subject happens to be. Kids need to be entertained nowadays. They need illustrations or photographs. Almost all of the books I've done in recent years contain as many pages of photographs as they do of text. It's not just books about sports that have been affected, of course. When I agreed to write a biography of Anwar Sadat for Walker & Company in 1981, the contract specified that I deliver, along with the manuscript, forty photographs of the Egyptian leader.

The writer as photographer

To be a successful free-lancer in the nonfiction field today, you have to know more than just how to write effective prose; you also have to be knowledgeable as to how and where you're going to obtain illustrative material to accompany the text. When I first began to realize the importance of illustrations in books for young readers, I took a course in photography and started buying equipment. I've found that taking my own photographs for my books is an enormous advantage, particularly when preparing instruction books. Specifically, I have in mind the series of "Better" books I've been writing for Dodd, Mead & Company—*Better Baseball for Boys, Better Roller Skating for Boys and Girls, Better Track for Girls,* etc. There are about thirty books in the series.

In taking my own photographs, I'm better able to blend the text and illustrative material for the benefit of the reader. For instance, when I was preparing a book on cross-country running not long ago, I had to explain that the runner's stride in cross-country usually involves planting the foot heel first. You can say, "Each foot should come down heel first as you stride," but the better way is to have a young and skilled runner, a trained member of a high school track team, run for you, and then take sequence photos of the runner as he or she passes in front of the camera lens. The final step is to pick out photos that show the heel-first stride most clearly.

The camera has been a boon to me in other ways. It gets me into places that I'd never be able to penetrate as a writer. Over the past few years, I've done a series of books, also for Dodd, Mead, that have sought to explain different pro sports for the young reader. They discuss each sport's beginnings, examine basic strategy, and profile a handful of the leading players. *This Is Pro Football* and *This Is Pro Soccer* are two of the books in the series. These books involved attending professional games, interviewing players and officials, and being a careful observer in an effort to get some behind-the-scenes idea of what was going on. If I had applied for press credentials as a writer, I would have been permitted to sit in the press box and watch what was taking place from there. But as a photographer, you have to be close to the action, so your credentials allow you to be on the field during the game, on the sidelines. In baseball, field photographers are posted in a small booth or dugout that's adjacent to the players' dugout.

You see and hear more when you're on the field. From the stands or on television, pro football often looks like a big shoving match. But when you watch a game from the sidelines, it's much different. You hear the shouts and grunts. You see the pain on the players' faces. You see the bruised flesh and blood. On the field, pro football is a violent game, a brutal game. I've tried to convey that aspect of the game to the reader.

The evolution toward the use of illustrative material in non-fiction books for young readers has culminated in such books as *A Very Young Gymnast* and *A Very Young Rider* by Jill

Krementz. These have scores of pictures, many of them half-page or full-page in size, but the text could have been prepared on the back of an envelope. I don't mean to sound pejorative; it's just what's happened.

Book packaging

I want to return briefly to those sports biographies that Putnam's used to publish. I remember how really happy I was the first time I signed a contract to do one of them, and not merely because it meant a check. Other writers in the series included Charles Einstein, Ray Robinson, Al Silverman, and the aforementioned Frank Graham. They were very solid writers, excellent craftsmen, experienced in writing articles as well as books. It made me feel good to join their company.

I mention this because I think it is less likely that today's nonfiction book for young readers is written by a committed professional. One reason for this is the advent of the book packager, the individual (or company) who contracts with a publisher to deliver one or an entire series of completed books, or at least camera-ready copy and art. The publisher becomes essentially a distributor.

In addition, I don't believe that the author of a packaged book feels a direct commitment to a publisher or to a particular group of readers. He or she is writing to satisfy the needs and demands of the packager, and that is much different. I know that when I write a book, I write it for my editor and for the readers that editor represents. We have a mutual understanding of what those readers are like.

The basic reason that packagers usually aren't able to attract top-level professionals is because they don't pay professional rates. They *can't*; it's the nature of the packaging business to pay less. Offers to writers from book packagers often amount to about one-half of accepted standard rates. Most packagers seek to have the writer work for a flat fee, that is, with no share in the royalties. If packagers paid their authors—and their editors and production people—standard rates, they would be paying what publishers paid, and they would have nothing left for themselves.

Packaged nonfiction books usually have great dazzle. They jump off the shelves. But they're often lacking in quality and substance.

I often question some of them from the standpoint of integrity. For example, many sports books today are packaged by NFL Properties, the marketing arm of the National Football League, or by the Major League Baseball Promotion Company. A book about football assembled by the NFL is something like a book about automobiles written by the people at Chevrolet.

Take football history as an example. You can't expect a book about football history that has been prepared by writers and editors representing the National Football League to credit *college* football coaches or players with any significant contribution to the game's development. You can't expect NFL writers and editors to speak objectively about competitive football leagues. Indeed, the records of one formerly competitive league, the American Football League, have been obliterated from professional football history.

This is not a fateful matter, I agree. It's merely typical of what can happen. What bothers me is that publishers generally accept whatever material they receive from the packager without question. They put their name on it and turn it over to the sales department.

At some major publishing firms, the basic attitudes toward books and bookselling have changed drastically in recent years. Books are no longer referred to as such. They are called the "product." And the idea of the publishing house is to "market the product." At some publishers, marketing has come to have precedence over writing and editing.

The Taboos

One of the leading features of young adult book publishing during the 1970s was the emergence of adult themes in nonfiction (and in fiction, too, of course). For I guess what was the first time, an author could find a welcome market for a book about divorce, or teenage pregnancy, or a dozen other such topics. "I guess about all the taboos have been broken," an editor said to me recently. I shook my head in reply. There are still plenty of topics that editors shy away from.

Burt Reynolds, for instance. In February each year, the Gallup Youth Survey of Princeton, New Jersey, publishes the results of a poll that the firm takes to find the "Most Admired Man" and "Most Admired Woman" in America. Burt Reynolds always winds up at or near the top of the men's list. It happens year in and year out. Teenage boys hold him in higher esteem than teenage girls do, according to Gallup.

And in December 1981, when *The World Almanac and Book of Facts* asked 2,000 eighth graders to name the thirty individuals they most admired and wanted to be like, Burt Reynolds ended up in the number 1 position. (Not a single business figure, government official, scientist, or world leader was in the top thirty.)

Why doesn't someone publish a Burt Reynolds biography for teenagers? I don't mean a biography that is filled with press-agent puffery or the type of information found in the pages of *People*. I mean a straightforward account of the man's life that would seek to give some insight into him and his career.

I'm not interested in writing such a book. I don't have any particular feeling toward Burt Reynolds, except that I marvel at his exceptional popularity among young people. I recently suggested a Burt Reynolds biography to a young adult book editor. I wanted to see how she would react. She looked at me if I had asked for a five-figure advance and unlimited expenses. For reasons that I don't have space to investigate here, Burt Reynolds is a taboo subject. So is Alan Alda, who also always ranks high in those popularity polls. So are most rock stars.

During the 1970s, when I was writing those sports biographies and much other sports nonfiction, and a dozen other authors were, too, I often wondered why no one was writing about popular music for the young adult market. Music is a much more popular subject than sports. I'm sure a biography of Michael Jackson would have been more successful than my book about Roger Staubach. Some teenage girls might have read it. As far as I know, the Roger Staubach biography never attracted any female readers.

I ran into another taboo early in the 1980s, when I began to realize how many millions of young people were playing videogames and decided I wanted to write a book about them. The *New York Times* said that videogames were so popular that they had helped to cripple the record industry and had overtaken motion pictures in terms of gross profits. The book I wanted to do had the working title *The Story of Video Games*. It was to tell how the games happened to come into existence, offer detailed information on their electronics and how they worked, and speculate on what they might be leading to in the future.

I had great difficulty trying to sell the idea, at least at first. Editors recoiled at the sight of my outline. Videogames were not a suitable subject for a teenage book, I was told. The topic was "too controversial." I kept trying, and eventually I came to an agreement with Frederick Warne & Company to publish the book. I feel certain it is going to be very successful.

I have a feeling that hardcover books for teenagers have to be more concerned with their likes and dislikes. I realize that publishers hesitate in contracting to publish a book about a popular favorite in the entertainment world. They're afraid that by the time the book is written, edited, printed, and distributed, no one will have any idea who the individual is any more. That's an argument that's heard frequently. But it seems as though I've been hearing about Burt Reynolds and Michael Jackson for a dozen or so years. In other words, it is possible to choose individuals whose careers are not going to evaporate overnight. Publishing such biographies would remove one more taboo.

The Bestseller

Another important trend in young adult books is a direct outgrowth of the many mergers that beset the publishing industry during the decade of the 1970s. Companies that were devoured by big corporations—Putnam's by MCA and Universal and Simon & Schuster by Gulf and Western, to name only two—seem much less interested in publishing books for the young adult market, indeed, for libraries, in general, than they used to be.

Part of the problem is economic, of course. Books for libraries are largely hardcover books, and most big publishers are reluctant to keep hardcover books in their warehouses, certainly not those that are not going to sell in important quantities. It's simply too expensive to do so, not only in terms of heat, light, salaries, and all the rest, but also in terms of the amount of capital that those books represent.

But that's only part of the problem. The editors who represent many publishers now owned by big corporations think chiefly in terms of bestsellers. Libraries and the relatively small print orders that the library market represents have little appeal to them.

In 1976, Frederick Warne published a book of mine entitled *Understanding Hydroponics*, an explanation of the science of growing plants in water containing nutrients, rather than soil. A couple of years earlier, Westminster Press published *How Does It Get There?*, a book I wrote that examined modern transportation methods. Dodd, Mead once published a book of mine that traced the history of lotteries in America. (Lottery tickets supported the Virginia Company's colonization efforts at Jamestown, and George Washington once conducted a private lottery.) All of these books were worthwhile. All contained information that couldn't help but be of interest to many young readers, information not readily available elsewhere. The books sold well, and they are still in print.

But fewer and fewer companies want to publish books of this type. Most big publishers, at least those that are members of conglomerates, want such books as the *ET Puzzle and Game Book*. There's nothing wrong with puzzle-and-game books. But they should be balanced by books of merit and substance.

An Ever-Changing Field

I enjoy writing for young readers. I really can't imagine myself doing anything else. But it's a field in which you have to keep alert.

I was really quite reluctant to write this essay. So many changes occur so fast in young adult publishing that it's difficult to make any general statement about the field and expect it to have any lasting relevance. What's taken as gospel truth in January can easily sound ludicrous by June. Book publishing for young adults reminds me of a statement about New York City that is often attributed to New York cabdrivers—"It's going to be a great city if they ever get through working on it."

7

The Trappings of Morality: Didacticism and the Young Adult Novel

MARILYN KAYE

Didacticism is a dirty word. When we describe a book as didactic, we're usually trying to say that it's moralistic and preachy, that it's attempting to instruct young people as to what they should do, think, say, be. The didactic story imposes values, mores, standards of behavior. The didactic story has a message.

In a sense, however, because all literature attempts to communicate something, all literature is didactic. Themes are frequently a sort of message. From a literary viewpoint, didacticism becomes a negative quality when the message overwhelms the story, and when instruction takes precedence over artistry. What it all boils down to is the intent of the author as we perceive it. Does the author appear to have as a main goal the expression of some sort of advice or guidance? Do all elements of the story—characterization, plot, theme—serve to accentuate and emphasize the message? Does the story appear only to provide a frame for a clearly apparent statement?

The Didactic Tradition

It is a commonly held assumption that literature reflects the society in which it is written. The history of young adult literature offers much evidence of the desire of an adult to pass on to the young the social values and mores of the period. Young adult literature is a relatively new literary phenomenon, but it too has a tradition of didacticism. When Maureen Daly's *Seventeenth Summer* was published in 1942, there was every indication that a fresh, vibrant literature for young adults was a real possibility. But the promise of *Seventeenth Summer* went unfulfilled, for most of what followed showed little evidence of the qualities for which that refreshingly honest romance was hailed. The young adult romance, in particular, degenerated into a rigid format that lacked substance. There were exceptions, of course—notably, Mary Stolz, whose provocative explorations of relationships demonstrated keen insight and artistic integrity.

Generally, however, a formula evolved, which could be easily perceived in the works of such prolific authors as Betty Cavanna and Rosamund du Jardin. These stories tended to center around a teenage girl's desire for a romantic involvement, a process frequently hindered by some personality problem, such as shyness, insecurity, lack of self-esteem, whatever. In her attempts to secure a successful relationship, her hang-ups would set in motion behavior that would ultimately create a conflict. For example, her insecurity might make her behave in an artificial manner. Her lack of self-esteem might cause her to set her sights on the "wrong" sort of boy. There were numerous variations-on-a-theme in these books, but in the end the girl would find herself happily ensconced in a pleasant (but not too serious) relationship, with the additional benefit of having learned a little something about herself in the process.

These weren't bad stories, and they did reflect some common adolescent trials and tribulations, even if the inevitable happy endings were a bit contrived. Why, then, did they seem so didactic? The messages were clearly apparent: Be yourself, don't do anything you'll be ashamed of later, don't make permanent romantic commitments, do listen to your parents (they know more about life than you do), don't succumb to peer pressure, and so forth. As far as sexual activity was concerned, there were fewer warnings, mainly because sexual desire was rarely acknowledged and thus there was little in the way of sexual conflict.

The message came through loud and clear mainly because of the format in which they thrived. The simplistic, predictable plots, the undistinguished writing, and the broad characterizations created a literary environment in which didacticism could flourish. Messages easily overwhelmed the stories since the stories themselves were so trivial. There were no revelations, no surprises, no interesting turns of events. Most significantly, there were no ambiguities. The problems were clearly stated and neatly resolved, and the conclusions left nothing open to the reader's interpretation. Characters were stylized, watered-down versions of "typical" adolescents. Real-life young adult readers were supposed to identify with these adolescent prototypes and share the characters' experiences, and thus, whatever the characters in these novels learned, the readers would accept as appropriate for themselves. But in what seemed to be attempts to create characters with whom any reader could identify, the end results were bland caricatures who were neither interesting nor memorable.

The New Realism of the Sixties

In the 1960s, the social upheaval in the United States provided the impetus for a dramatic new style in literature written especially for young adults. The 1960s were a time of awakening, a time in which the collective consciousness was rising and expanding. Traditions were questioned. Issues were confronted. There was a spirit in the air, a spirit that opened the doors to a new awareness, and a reevaluation of what had long been passively accepted.

The young adult novel as a literary form had new options. Topics once considered taboo could be examined. For the romantic novel, especially, aspects of social change had enormous impact. Increasingly liberal attitudes regarding premarital sexual activities, feminism, the gay rights movement—all contributed to an expanded view of the nature of romance. Young adult novels began dealing with more complex ideas and situations, which required a more sophisticated approach. For the romantic novel, this meant a serious consideration of the many implications that accompanied these more liberal attitudes.

How did this infusion of new topics and new considerations affect the didactic nature of the literature? Obviously, there would be new messages since there were new problems. Young people now had more options in the way of romantic expression. The lifting of old taboos and the willingness to discuss aspects of romance once considered immoral or unacceptable set a stage in which easy solutions were no longer available. There were new moral issues to confront. Given the option to engage freely in premarital sexual relations, young people faced the responsibility of creating their own moral code and a slew of questions: Should I or shouldn't I? How? With whom? Why?

Unlike the types of problems posed in earlier romantic novels, these questions did not lend themselves to snappy, upbeat, and predictable answers. We were a society in a state of flux. Traditional precise moral codes no longer seemed realistic—but there were no new precise moral codes to take the place of the old rules and regulations. Earlier, authors could speak confidently when they offered advice as to how a proper, socially acceptable romance should be conducted. There were specific mainstream values that could be communicated to the young through the portrayal of a typical adolescent resolving a typical conflict in a manner that was quite obviously appropriate. By the end of the 1960s, however, and continuing to this day, the notion of "mainstream values" had faded. Controversies over such issues as sex education, free birth-control guidance, legal abortion, the Equal Rights Amendment, and the rights of homosexuals were evidence of a nation with no general social consensus as to what was morally right or wrong.

This state of moral ambiguity and dissension has worked to the advantage of young adult fiction. As life got tougher, so did the literature. In the past, fictional romantic problems led to conflicts, which led to solutions—and the solution could then be translated into a message for the reader. The contemporary romantic novel also deals with problems that lead to conflicts; but without a generally accepted moral code to provide an easy solution.

The new didacticism

I'm not saying that the advent of the new realism rang the death bell for didacticism. In some ways, the new realism also provided the scope for an even stronger didacticism than we had previously encountered. Although the best of the new writers took advantage of the new range of topics by exploring their implications and ramifications, other writers exploited

these topics to express a social viewpoint. Since these viewpoints related to controversial topics, and since there was no
general social consensus as to the morality of various issues,
writers who wished to convey a message had to make that message very clear; and the resulting novels were highly didactic.

For example, take a look at one of the more controversial
novels of the period, Judy Blume's *Forever*. With all the
hullabaloo over the mildly explicit sexual scenes, it was easy
to overlook the fact that the story is actually a very moral
one—moral to a fault. In fact, the book is highly reminiscent of
the romances of twenty to thirty years ago. The only real difference is in its contemporary moral setting. In *Forever*, we
have wise adults offering sage counsel; negative examples in
the form of girls who have sex for the "wrong" reasons (that is,
reasons based on something other than mutual affection); and a
protagonist who learns that a first love should not result in a
permanent commitment. If you take the actual sex out of
Forever, and replace it with "going steady," you have a classic
romantic young adult novel—with all the messages intact.

One kind of didacticism that emerged from the new realism
incorporated an explicit rejection of traditional values. For example, the heroine of Norma Klein's *It's OK If You Don't Love
Me* is violently "modern"; she's so innately liberated that she
responds with total bewilderment to any mention of traditional sex role behavior. In Sandra Scoppettone's *Trying Hard
to Hear You*, a heroine reacts with dismay to the discovery of a
friend's homosexuality. The author then uses this heroine to
demonstrate to the reader how the heterosexual *should* respond to homosexuality and instructs the reader as to the development of sensitivity, understanding, and acceptance. In
another Scoppettone work, *Happy Endings Are All Alike*, the
lesbian heroine is a throwback to an earlier period: She's an
idealized representation of a "type." Singlehandedly, she over-
throws all stereotyped images, consoles and advises those who
are bewildered by her sexual orientation, instructs the ignorant
as to the "true" nature of homosexuality, and fights hypocrisy
and prudery—not to mention the fact that she's beautiful, in-
telligent, well-meaning, and an all-around exemplary human
being. She may serve as a standard, an ideal of female homosexuality; but is she a believable character?

There's nothing wrong with the values these works are presenting. To be honest, I find myself in sympathy with authors
who attempt to show readers a way of looking at life that's con-

sistent with my own attitude. But, at the same time, how do we rank these works as literature? Our background in evaluation tells us to be wary of literature that's message-laden. Does it matter, then, whether the messages come out of a conservative, complacent value system or whether they come out of a new liberal order that's in tune with our own way of thinking?

One of our problems in evaluating literature for young adults now is based on the fact that we are so much more conscious of the stereotypes, omissions, and misrepresentations of the past. For so long young adult books treated adolescents as if their lives were carefree, their problems negligible; now some authors seem to be trying to make up for that by giving adolescents every serious problem imaginable. And we carefully examine each and every novel for any hint of those infamous "isms": sex, race, age, handicap—you name it. In efforts to eradicate the stereotypes associated with various groups, some authors make fervent attempts to present not only a rejection of the stereotype but a superpositive image of a member of that group. Certainly, it is right and appropriate to dismiss myth-laden false group characteristics. All women (as a group) are not exclusively committed to home and family. Elderly people (as a group) are not senile. Handicapped people (as a group) are not helpless. But—it is also false to assume that not one person from these groups can ever exhibit one of these characteristics. There are critics and reviewers and librarians who assume that the presentation of one forgetful elderly person in one novel is an indication of ageism, or that the portrayal of a contented housewife with no career aspirations is sexist. This attitude seems to be based on the assumption that any one character in a novel is representative of all people of that character's age, sex, race, etc. This attitude promotes and encourages a didactic tone in novels. Frequently, the novel that incorporates this attitude presents a vision of life as it should be, not life as it is.

What has been particularly disturbing in the past decade is the expressed desire on the part of some critics for *more* didacticism. In a March 1976 article in *Wilson Library Bulletin* entitled "Can Young Gays Find Happiness in YA Books?," the authors criticized a group of novels for their treatments of gay characters, and stated that in none of the novels discussed do protagonists "go on to find fulfillment and a supportive relationship based on love and respect." The authors implied that it was the responsibility of each novelist to present a positive image of homosexuality and that the work of fiction should answer informational questions about the subject. They specifically requested that the novels present "role models," and that the novels offer standards and ideals of behavior. They questioned the existence of persecution in these novels, and asked ". . . in an open democratic society, why must minorities be expected to withstand extraordinary pressures?" Perhaps because, in real life, they do.

This article is just one example. I've heard a novel criticized for its inclusion of a minor character, an uneducated black woman in the role of a maid. I've heard another novel criticized for its portrayal of a macho, womanizing high school football player. These images are not pleasant to confront, and we may wish these situations did not exist in real life. But they do exist, and to pretend they don't means we're lying to ourselves and our readers. Not all black women are maids, and not all football players are macho; but some are. To ignore this is fuel for didacticism. We see evidence for this in the *Bulletin of the Council on Interracial Books for Children*, which judges books purely and solely on the basis of their didactic value through its exclusive emphasis on cultural images and the "lessons" to be learned from the literature.

The nondidactic novel

Happily, though, there have been many authors who have risen high above the traps available in the new realism and who concentrate on perceptive, penetrating explorations of youth in contemporary society. M. E. Kerr is a shining example. Her novels investigate the spirit and soul of adolescents, the meanings of love, the nature of relationships. She raises many questions, but she doesn't provide answers, which is right and appropriate, because the questions she asks do not have answers. She has focused on protagonists of unusual characteristics and circumstances in novels such as *Little Little* and *What I Really Think of You*. And readers can relate to these characters, despite the fact that they may not have any experience with dwarfs or evangelical religion. The readers are reached through the quality of emotion, the convincing expression of thought and action that can pull them into an unfamiliar situation and allow them to share it.

Fine writers like Kerr, Robert Cormier, S. E. Hinton, Robert Lipsyte, and many others have no need to rely on superficial character types to provide a means of reader identification.

We're very fortunate today to have for young adults an exciting body of literature, novels of lasting value that do not attempt to moralize or instruct.

Didacticism and Librarianship

But didacticism remains an ever-present danger, and all of us who care about literature and our adolescent clientele must be sensitive to its presence. Didacticism can be seductive. When a novel contains an explicit message with which we, as adults, agree, we may not see it as a negative quality. There are values that we want our young people to develop, and when a novel promotes these values we sometimes overlook the fact that these values are expressed in such a way that they are detrimental to the overall quality of a novel.

An overtly didactic novel demonstrates disrespect for the reader. It's sneaky and dishonest. It's propaganda. It candy-coats instruction. And it distorts our process of evaluation: Aesthetics become confused with politics, and the intrinsic complexity of values becomes trivialized.

What we want are stories. Rich, sensitive stories, with unique and convincing adolescent protagonists, drama, humor, satire, adventure, romance, provocative themes, lasting impressions. What we don't want are sermons and moral instruction disguised as fiction. The very best novels are open to interpretation and allow readers the right and the pleasure to draw their own conclusions. And as librarians, it is our right, our pleasure, and our obligation to make certain these novels are available to our readers.

8
Censorship Did Not End at Island Trees: A Look Ahead

NAT HENTOFF

In fall 1982, at a public library in rural Indiana, a book was missing: a scholarly history of homosexuality. One morning, as a librarian picked up the books that had been returned overnight through a slot in the door, she screamed: "Oh my God, they've killed this book!" In her hands was the volume on homosexuality, back home at last — with two bullets in it.

Around the same time, in Wise County, Virginia, a public school principal, yielding to the fierce complaints of some parents, removed *The Diary of Anne Frank* from the required reading list of a seventh-grade class. They said it was too graphic. (Some folks in town figured the real reason was that Anne Frank had shown scandalous disrespect for authority.) A story about the stigmatizing of the book appeared in the *Washington Post* and, as usually happens when the media call attention to acts of censorship, people in the town became quite embarrassed. No one likes to be seen as living in a town or a city full of yahoos. So the principal put *The Diary of Anne Frank* back on the required reading list.

In Torrance, California, also not long after the Supreme

Court's decision in the *Island Trees* case (more of which to come), some parents moved to protect their high school children, and all other students in the school, from George Orwell's *1984* and Ray Bradbury's *Fahrenheit 451*. They wanted the books removed from required reading lists because they're the kinds of books that make youngsters gloomy and suspicious.

Meanwhile, in Minnesota, around Christmas of the year of the *Island Trees* decision, two YA librarians told me that they were not going to buy any more books by Judy Blume. It wouldn't matter what the reviews were. It wouldn't matter how many requests there were for the books. Judy Blume is trouble. Her books agitate certain parents. And, these librarians said, "We don't need any more trouble." In Boulder, Colorado, a group of "concerned parents" anonymously circulated packets of what they consider to be pornographic materials from the collected works of the very same Judy Blume. The packets went to public school principals, to local ministers, and to other parents. One of the harmful Blume lines most heavily underlined by these watchful parents was: "Damn it, don't treat me like a child!"

The Island Trees Decision

Attempts at censorship—including preselection censorship—do not appear to have been much discouraged by the *Island Trees* decision. To understand why, it's useful to look closely at what the Supreme Court actually did say about books for young readers and the First Amendment—and also at what it did *not* say.

To begin with, the Court did hold, narrowly, that there is a First Amendment right to read. A majority of the Court had never said this explicitly before. Justice William Brennan calls this a right "to receive information and ideas." Where is this right to be found in the First Amendment? It is, says Brennan, "an inherent corollary of the rights of free speech and press that are explicitly guaranteed by the Constitution." That is, if you have the First Amendment right to send ideas, what's the point of it all unless there is a corollary First Amendment right of the people you're addressing to receive your ideas?

So that's an important victory, establishing the right to read. However, the Court, in *Island Trees*, put some rather severe limitations on that right—in a school setting. Remember, the case is about school libraries and what powers a school board has to remove books from those libraries. Within that carefully circumscribed area, the Court has declared that students and parents protesting what they consider acts of censorship in school libraries have a First Amendment right to go to court to try to prove that a particular book was removed because school authorities disliked or disagreed with the ideas in it. Under the First Amendment, a school library must include a diversity of ideas. There can't be an orthodoxy of thought on those library shelves.

It is not likely to be easy for students or parents to win such a case if the censoring authority is less than forthright about its motives. The Supreme Court, for instance, says there is no First Amendment protection, in this context, if a book is removed because it is "pervasively vulgar" or educationally unsuitable. Both those criteria are quite broad and can give a censor of ideas considerable leeway in disguising the true motivation.

In any case, it is, of course, important that the Court has established this First Amendment right to go to trial to determine the motivation of a school board that removed books from a library. However, the Court provides no relief for anyone who would challenge preselection censorship—those librarians in Minnesota, for instance, who have said "nevermore" to all future Judy Blume books. Said Brennan: "Nothing in our decision today affects in any way the discretion of a local school board to choose books to add to the libraries of their schools. Because we are concerned in this case with the suppression of ideas, our holding today affects only the discretion to remove books."

Justice William Rehnquist was one of the four dissenters, each of whom believes ardently that the courts should have no control over school board removal of books. But Rehnquist could not resist exposing Brennan's illogic in exempting preselection of books from the First Amendment involvement. Rehnquist said

The failure of a library to acquire a book denies access to its contents just as effectively as does the removal of the book from the library's shelf. . . . If a school board's removal of books might be motivated by a desire to promote favored political or religious views, there is no reason that its acquisition policy might not also be so motivated. And yet the "pall of orthodoxy"

*cast by a carefully selected book-acquisition program ap-
parently would not violate the First Amendment under Justice
Brennan's view.*

Brennan, in his plurality opinion, also left another very large
loophole for those who would cast a "pall of orthodoxy" over a
school. Justice Brennan emphasized that "the curricula of the
Island Trees schools" were not at issue in this case. "On the
contrary," Brennan said, "the only books at issue in this case are
library books, books that by their nature are optional rather
than required reading. Our adjudication of the present case
thus does not intrude into the classroom, or into the compul-
sory course taught there."

Another dissenter, Chief Justice Warren Burger, took mock-
ing delight in pointing up Justice Brennan's illogic in allowing
this second loophole: "It would appear that required reading
and textbooks have a greater likelihood of imposing a 'pall of
orthodoxy' over the educational process than do optional
reading [in the school library]."

So parents and others who strive to purge required reading
lists of unorthodox books have been told by the Court that
they can continue their cleansing work with impunity. It is
worth noting, by the way, that during the strenuous efforts
around the country in recent years to expel *Huckleberry Finn*
from public schools because of Mark Twain's "racism"—an
upside-down reading of the novel (most of the novel)—a majority of the complaints were directed at the required reading lists
on which the book had been placed.

As Warren Burger points out, permitting censorship of classroom materials does not fit very comfortably with Justice Brennan's assertion that books can't be removed from library
shelves in order to "prescribe what shall be orthodox in
politics, nationalism, religion, or other matters of opinion." It
amounts to allowing a "pall of orthodoxy" over one part of the
school and the First Amendment in another: a new form of
school segregation.

On occasion, moreover, the very same book will be given
First Amendment protection in the library while being kicked
out of class. In Island Trees, for instance, negotiations took
place after the Supreme Court decision as to what would happen to the nine books that had been removed by the school
board. (The board did not want to go to trial both because of the
added expense and also because residents of Island Trees, after

all the publicity about the case, were beginning to feel embarrassed at being taken for a bunch of backwoods knownothings.)

At first, the Island Trees school board said it would return the books to the library but would require that a notice be sent to the parent of each child who checked out any of those notorious volumes. The New York Civil Liberties Union lawyers for the student plaintiffs would have no part of this deal, because they had gone to court in the first place to fight the stigmatizing of books. The school board finally agreed that the books would go back on the library shelves, but one of them — Bernard Malamud's *The Fixer* — was to be punished elsewhere in the school. It had been on a required reading list when the trouble started, and the school board vowed that as long as it was in office, *The Fixer* would not be taught in any Island Trees classroom. The Supreme Court decision permits just this kind of second-class citizenship for a book in the classroom.

Other Attempts at Censorship

Some First Amendment lawyers predict that the Court, having now begun to deal, however gingerly, with the First Amendment interests in school library censorship, will eventually go on to consitutional issues involved in preselection and curriculum censorship. So it may, but in view of the close vote in *Island Trees* — and the explicit exemption of those two areas in Justice Brennan's decision — the odds are not high that First Amendment protections will be extended to these matters for some time to come.

In any case, there is surely going to be continuing preselection and curriculum censorship. Nor are attempts to remove books from school libraries going to stop. From now on, school boards will be more careful to present their most acceptable motivation for banning a book. Also, assaults on books in public libraries will not cease, for, as Phil Kerby, an editorial writer for the *Los Angeles Times*, put it: "Censorship is the strongest drive in human nature; sex, a weak second."

When a public library is besieged, the pressures are often more political than those of a courtroom combat. Library boards may waver and suppress a book in reaction to concentrated, sustained attack by a group in the community. Or those public officials in charge of deciding library funding may vote to impoverish a public library that refuses to jettison a controversial book.

Whatever the kind of library that finds itself under attack, the most effective ways of both sticking to principle and also surviving are basically the same for public libraries or school libraries. Following are some case histories.

The Washington County (Virginia) Library

A classic case in point concerns the battle, in Abingdon, Virginia, between public librarian Kathy Russell and a fundamentalist minister, the Reverend Tom Williams—along with Williams's political ally, Bobby Sproles, chairman of the Washington County Board of Supervisors.

Williams, apprised of the fact that the Washington County Library in Abingdon contained such licentious books as *The Lonely Lady* by Harold Robbins and *Bloodline* by Sidney Sheldon, marched into that library and asked for the names of all of its patrons who had checked out those and certain other books that he considered pornographic. The minister particularly wanted the names of minors who had been tainted by these volumes.

Kathy Russell said in response that she had always regarded the confidentiality of such information to be a fundamental protection for patrons of any public library. Nobody should be policing what people choose to read. Not in a free nation anyway. (Fortunately, for her, Virginia is one of a minority of states that by statute specifically forbids disclosing records that identify a library user and the material borrowed by that user.)

From the very beginning of this library battle of Armageddon with Reverend Williams, Kathy Russell made sure that her answers to every one of his accusations and demands were made immediately available to the print and broadcast press. She never let the opposition's charges accumulate to the point where she was defensively submerged.

For instance, in her comments to the newspaper, radio, and television reporters, Russell continually countered the reverend's assertions that she was nurturing groves of pornography in that deeply conservative—politically and religiously—county. The accused books, she said, were guilty of being bestsellers, as listed in the *New York Times*, but were otherwise innocent of any criminality. Then Reverend Williams retorted that the books were seen as pornographic by a good many folks in Washington County, and their tax money should not be spent on materials that offend their moral sensibilities.

As it happened, Kathy Russell responded, each of the books he wanted to banish had been purchased by the library "only after a number of requests for the book had been received by citizens who were regular patrons of the library. They pay taxes too," said the librarian. Furthermore, in her interviews and in her calm, lucid, precise letters to the media, Russell pointed to the American Library Association's Bill of Rights — particularly to: "While anyone is free to reject books for himself, he cannot exercise the right of censorship to restrict the freedom to read of others."

After awhile, the librarian's clarity and sureness of principle had won over the Kiwanis Club of Abingdon, which passed a resolution urging the library board to resist the censors and to continue to provide reading materials for the county's "diverse citizenry."

Most revealingly, in the county's newspapers, the dailies and the weeklies, Kathy Russell got more and more support as the war continued — in editorials, and most tellingly, in letters to the editor, of which there was a huge quantity. It was as if the spirits of Madison and Jefferson had returned to their native Virginia and had regenerated a passion for liberty in their descendants.

Wrote one resident of Abingdon to the *Washington County News:*

This is too much. Way too much. It is time to react to this outrageous impudence and let the self-righteous bigots know that we will not further tolerate having them decide for us what we shall read and what we shall not. . . . No one forces these morality experts to go in any book store or library and read a single word that offends them: what right have they to assume that because something is offensive to them personally that the material must be proscribed for the rest of us. . . . Get off our backs. You read what you want and let me and others read what we want.

Another furious citizen wrote: "While I am NOT defending pornography, I AM defending my right to read what I please, and I'll be damned if Mr. Sproles or Mr. Williams are going to tell me that because they don't like certain books, others cannot read them."

Yet another citizen-reader touched on that part of the First

Amendment that separates church and state: "If I wanted to submit to Reverend Williams's moral influence, I would attend his church. I do not. Yet, he wants to stretch his long arm from the pulpit of that church through the door of the library and yank books from their shelves. This is simply not right."

There was also a warning by a columnist, Lowry Bowman of the *Washington County News:* "Editorial thunder cannot supplant the first duty of citizens. If a majority of citizens is willing to have someone else dictate what they may read, what they may do, that's the way it will be."

That was indeed the most fundamental point of the conflict, and Kathy Russell had made it clear to the press and to the citizens. And when the citizens came to also see that Reverend Williams was trying to take away their right to decide for themselves what they would read, Kathy Russell's support grew and grew. And the books under attack stayed on the shelves.

At the beginning of the fight, Russell, twenty-three, was rather shy and so soft-spoken that it was hard to hear her unless you were right next to her. Over the months, while she remained decidedly nonabrasive, the librarian became more confident as a speaker and more sure of herself altogether. "It was kind of difficult at times," she told me. "You know, those times when you're by yourself, and you really do wonder what's going to happen. But I did what I had to do. As a librarian, I had no choice."

Early on, one of the statements she made—to the *Bristol Herald Courier*—had considerable impact. This Library-Bill-of-Rights theme may be commonplace to librarians, but it is not so well known to the citizenry at large, and therefore it's vital that this point be made widely known:

It would conflict with the public interest for the library to establish its own political, moral, or artistic views, or to enforce the views of any single group in the community as the standard for determining what materials should be made available [emphasis added]. Moreover, it is the responsibility of librarians in the United States to make available materials representing all points of view concerning the questions and issues of our time and reflecting all tastes.

And later, to a reporter from the *Richmond Times-Dispatch*— as the Reverend Williams kept trying to awaken the countryside to the dangers of pornography—Russell emphasized that a library cannot exclude books because a group of citizens unilaterally decides they're pornographic. Indeed, she said, there are books that offend people, but "it would be chilling if you had to base your selection of books on what suited everybody."

The Oak Lawn (Illinois) Public Library

Elsewhere in the nation, whenever censorship wars have attracted press attention, and the issues have been made clear by the embattled librarian, most of the citizens wind up supporting their own right to read—as in Oak Lawn, a suburb southwest of Chicago, during a long, fierce battle over whether the book *Show Me* should be in the Oak Lawn Public Library. There too, as the issue became clear, the First Amendment grew personal to many people in the community who had never really examined the dynamics of censorship. A local insurance agent in Oak Lawn, for instance, told a reporter: "After awhile, people took the attitude: 'Who has the right to tell me what book I may or may not show to my kids?' "

The Montello (Wisconsin) school libraries

And in Montello, Wisconsin, a small town northeast of Madison, it looked for awhile as if a group called Concerned Citizens would get away with a raid on the high school and elementary school libraries, during which they took from the shelves thirty-three books they had unilaterally decided were unfit for student consumption.

Among the titles were such of the usual suspects as *Catcher in the Rye, Catch-22*, James Baldwin's *Nobody Knows My Name*, Claude Brown's *Manchild in the Promised Land*, and of course, two of Judy Blume's progeny, *Are You there, God? It's Me Margaret* and *Starring Sally J. Friedman as Herself*. I was not surprised to see *Rights of Students* on the list, as well as Paul Goodman's *Growing Up Absurd*, a classic dissection of kindless education. Also included was *The Diary of Anne Frank*.

Lest anyone think they were common thieves, Concerned Citizens left in place of the books they took a bunch of religious tracts. And they also soon let it be known that they certainly were not censors but rather were engaged in "screening" books to protect the children from material that is profane, sexually explicit, or provides "negative portrayals" of life in the United States or in American history.

In this respect, Concerned Citizens of Montello shared a concern with the concerned school board of Island Trees. One of the books banned by the latter was Alice Childress's *A Hero Ain't Nothing but a Sandwich*. The reason: A character in that book said, accurately, that the father of our country, George Washington, owned slaves.

Following the raid on the school libraries, Concerned Citizens decided to put up some candidates for the imminent school board election. Joining forces on the other side were librarians, teachers, and other citizens with a certain affection for the First Amendment. What helped decide the race was the effect of publicity on the voters—first statewide and then national—connected with the kidnapping of thirty-three books for the greater good of the children.

As print reporters and television crews (some of the latter from CBS and NBC) came into the town, the majority of the local residents got the very unpleasant feeling that they were being portrayed as a collection of provincials, of yahoos, of censors. Said a seventeen-year-old Montello High School senior in disgust: "It's like this is turning into an X-rated place or something." Said Gene Conrad, editor of the *Marquette County Tribune:* "The impression is that this community is full of nothing but red-necks and Neanderthals. . . . It's my feeling the community will not stand for this. I know I won't editorially."

The books were returned to the school libraries; and Concerned Citizens was defeated in the school board election—despite the boldly clarifying assertion by one of its candidates that "It is not censorship to replace one book with another."

Still, a librarian in the town is fearful that it could happen again, with opposite results. "What's been taking place," she says, "is frightening for anybody who cares about students. And it is personal to anybody who believes that the First Amendment exists." What most worries this librarian is that there don't seem to be too many adults to whom the First Amendment is personal.

The Enemy Within

After all, in a Gallup poll a few years ago, three of every four Americans drew a blank when asked if they knew what was in the First Amendment to the Constitution. And of those Americans with a college background, six out of every ten registered a blank when asked the same question.

Even some librarians do not seem to regard the First Amendment as all that personal. For instance, preselection censorship may be permitted by the *Island Trees* decision, but it is censorship nonetheless, and it would appear to be widely practiced.

At the July 1982 convention of the American Library Association in Philadelphia, a questionnaire was widely distributed. It had been prepared by the Young Adult Services Intellectual Freedom Committee. Among the questions on the questionnaire were:

———— Have you not purchased teenage sex books from a conservative religious point of view, such as *How to Be Happy Though Young*, because a staff member found them personally repugnant? . . .

———— Have you not purchased a popular young adult title such as [Judy Blume's] *Forever* because it might be unpopular with parents? . . .

———— Have you reviewed potentially controversial materials and recommended that they not be purchased because of poor characterization, poorly developed plot, or due to other violations of the "Law of Literary Merit," even though there are other *noncontroversial* materials already in the collection that also violate the "Law of Literary Merit"?

A good many librarians were filling out the questionnaires with a rather embarrassed air. Self-censorship, which is another name for preselection censorship, is the easiest way to avoid trouble. No one's watching. Certainly not the press. There's no way they'll know about it.

On the other hand, there are librarians, a goodly number, who base their professional lives on the principle distilled in the American Library Association 1953 credo, *The Freedom to Read:* "We believe . . . that what people read is deeply important; that ideas can be dangerous; but that suppression of ideas is fatal to a democratic society. Freedom itself is a dangerous way of life, but it is ours." And those are the librarians who—more than any other group in this nation, including journalists—have persistently been the most resplendent and sometimes heroic, champions of free speech and press in recent years. Among them: Kathy Russell, Virginia; Jeanne Layton, Utah; Sonja Coleman, Massachusetts; Susan Maasz, Wisconsin; and Irene Turin, New York.

Irene Turin was and is a librarian in Island Trees, and from the very beginning she spoke out against the school board's censorship of the school library books. She also provided encouragement and support to the students who were also protesting—some of whom became the plaintiffs in this historic First Amendment suit. Because she would not bend, Irene Turin was often treated by the school board and school administrators as if she were a nonperson. Yet she stayed. She felt, she says, that "it was important for kids to know that there are adults who care about the freedom to read and about free speech. Adults who care enough to put themselves at risk."

It is one thing for students—including adults—to read of legendary American figures who kept liberty alive in this nation by taking risks to defend it. It is quite another thing—and much more emboldening because it is so immediately real—to actually see someone in your own community to whom the First Amendment is compellingly personal. Increasingly, librarians have taken on that role. And more are needed. As a librarian in Minnesota says, "I wish professionals would become more courageous. I realize there are jobs on the line. But being courageous is the most important role we can play. Because if we don't, who will?"

Island Trees is not the promised land, but it is a beginning. How much farther we go depends on the need and spirit of those who have chosen books as a way of life. A few months after *Island Trees*, at a meeting of the New York Library Association in Albany, a research librarian told her colleagues:

Many of you will never get involved in a large-scale external censorship battle with Moral Majority or with a group of feminists who want to remove books that abound with stereotypes of women. But every one of you will be involved in preselection decisions. How you deal with these decisions can do much more damage to the integrity of your collection than an open brawling free-speech fight with the television lights on and a microphone in your face.

Kathy Russell only had a fundamentalist minister to deal with. Librarians, however, sometimes have to cope with a much more knowledgeable opponent—the enemy within.

9
Booktalking

RHONNA GOODMAN

In any community, no matter how small or how grand the public library may be, it is essential for a committed library staff to have a fully developed outreach program for teenagers. Outreach can be accomplished in many different ways, including reference and referral, job and career counseling, and programming. However, the single most important outreach technique is booktalking. A time-honored method of reaching young people, it is as effective and as easy to accomplish in times of retrenchment as during times of affluence. It can be done by a professional staff of twenty or more or by a single practitioner. Love of books, respect for teenagers, and the willingness to share with young adults the fun of reading are the needed qualities.

Arranging for the Class Visit

In many communities, there has never been a formal channel for class visits by a public librarian. The argument is that the school librarian takes care of all the young people's reading needs at the junior high and high school levels. But, in many cases, the school librarian is so busy teaching the basic library skills program required by most boards of education that there is little time left for the booktalking/recreational class.

Because the school librarian is responsible for fostering reading and research skills in the school, it is preferable to have her or him sponsor the booktalk program. If this is not possible because of problems with the school's scheduling structure, the person in charge of English classes should be approached.

In some cases, there may be resistance from the school to allow the public librarian in or the classes out. The school administration may not believe that there is anything of importance in the public library presentation, or the school librarian may feel threatened or feel that the public librarian's program is superfluous. If resistance is strong, it may be necessary for the public library director to approach either the principal or the school board for permission. But first, plan a campaign. Be as cooperative as possible with the schools. Prepare book lists, put assignment books on reference shelves, offer the library as a showcase for artwork or writing contests, and plan cooperative programs, such as providing reading list books at the library during the summer.

Preparing for Booktalks

Preparing for booktalks is arduous and time consuming, but there is nothing like that feeling of accomplishment, or "high," from having successfully related to the young people and encouraged them to develop an interest in the public library and in good books.

1. Begin by reading a large variety of books suitable to the age and reading level of the class. Remember not all books are suitable to booktalking. Books with lots of action or many episodes are best for beginners.
2. Focus on an incident from the book—preferably from the beginning.
3. Write out the talk and read it aloud. It should not be more than three to four minutes long.
4. The secret is to be completely familiar with the talk, yet ap-

pear spontaneous: Practice—over and over—in the shower, in front of the mirror, in front of friends, in the car, etc.

5. Beginners have a tendency to ramble, so stick to a time schedule and have a prepared conclusion.

6. Keep a file of your written booktalks. Also, whenever you read a book, jot down the events that might make a good booktalk, and keep such notes in the file, as well. This will save an enormous amount of work later.

The Library Class

The most desirable location for booktalking is the public library itself. The librarian is at ease in his or her own environment, and the young people welcome the chance to be out of the school classroom.

The class should be invited to come to the library either at a time of the day when the library is closed or during a slow time of day. If the library is closed, chairs can be set up near the young adult section; a pleasant auditorium can also be used but is less desirable. The children's area or the story-hour room should be avoided. However, if it is the only seating space available, remove the picture books that may be opened and on display and replace them with hard-core YA materials. Be sure to explain to the class that this is the only available space.

When the class files in, have the students remove their coats and hats and put their books and other equipment under their chairs. On a table in front of the class, attractively arrange ten or so different books that are on the general reading level of the class. Include some large, visually attractive books on unusual subjects (such as robots, animals, or cheerleading), as well as paperback fiction and popular nonfiction. Also have a record or two, cassettes, videodiscs, and other materials the library circulates.

The booktalks

Plan the formal presentation to be no more than twenty minutes long. Know the reading level of the class, and plan well in advance. Generally, a class in a library should include talks on no more than three or four books, with the other books on display to show the range of materials available.

1. Before you begin the booktalks, explain that you are the young adult librarian, the person who works specially with teenagers, and that you would like to tell them about the library and about some books that you think they might enjoy.

2. Don't begin until the audience settles down. While waiting, smile and look friendly.

3. Start with a book that is of universal appeal (the surefire book) to all the students in the classroom. Leave an unusual book for the end, when the class trusts you and knows that this is a pleasurable experience.

4. Start and finish with author and title.

5. Try to connect the books in some way (thematic booktalks are not as successful in a recreational setting).

6. Have a large variety of books present during the talks.

7. Any book talked about must be allowed to circulate. Try to have duplicate copies of each book.

At times, a short film can be included as part of the presentation. The film should always be presented after the booktalks. Even the most experienced and expert booktalker can't compete with a film.

The do's and don'ts of booktalking

Booktalking has been dealt with quite thoroughly in Joni Bodart's fine book *Booktalking!* (H. W. Wilson, 1980) and in "Booktalking, You Can Do It!" by Mary K. Chelton (*School Library Journal*, April 1976). Following is a list of do's and don'ts that summarizes my own personal technique of booktalking.

1. If the talk is not going over well, cut it short and go on to the next book. Do be flexible, because all kinds of things can happen.

2. Don't read. As soon as you do, you lose eye contact. But if you do use the author's words, don't memorize them—even poetry.

3. If possible, do use some of the author's words. Try to capture some of the author's descriptive techniques and make the characters come alive.

4. Speak clearly. Do not try to imitate accents, but change the voice level when doing a conversation. Don't be overly

dramatic, and don't use gestures: Stand with your hands in your pockets if necessary.

5. Don't just tell what the book is about, relay a specific incident—it is far more interesting—but don't tell the only exciting incident in the book.

6. Try to remember the characters' names. This can be particularly difficult when doing several junior novels. (If necessary, sneak a look at the book jacket.) But don't introduce too many characters; this can be confusing.

7. Don't use notes.

8. Don't use words that are suggestive or titillating. This can set off a group into embarrassed giggles.

9. Don't be judgmental about the book: Don't say things like "This is the funniest book I've read."

Remember, teenagers are harsh critics, but not nearly as harsh as you are about yourself. You will probably be nervous at the start, but the look of rapt attention on their faces will make you forget all your problems. Have fun!

Library information

Besides the booktalks, the library class should include the following information about the library: when the library is open, special events and programs, and unique services the library provides. Also, briefly describe the type of reference collection that is available, interlibrary loan, and the reserve system. Some people prefer to do all of the booktalks before going to library information; others like to intersperse library information between the booktalks. It usually takes several classes before a beginner decides on a style.

After the formal part of the class, individual reader's guidance can be done. Any problems that the young adults may have with the library (overdue books or lost books or cards) can be resolved on the spot. The class can also be introduced to other sections of the library, such as the recordings, microfilm in the reference department, or the microcomputer section. And, most important, the students can actually take out, then and there, any of the books that have been discussed. Be sure to alert the clerical staff that the class is coming; there should be enough staff to register the students for cards and to check out materials with ease.

The School Class

It is more often the rule that classes are too far from the library and time restrictions too severe for the class to come to the library. In those cases, the librarian goes to the school. Classes in the school incorporate much of what takes place in the library class; however, certain modifications have to be made.

Most schools want the class to cover an entire period—usually forty-five minutes. This means talks on six or more books (based on a three- to four-minute booktalk). It is best not to schedule more than two classes in one day: A librarian who is new to booktalking will find more than that exhausting, especially since there is probably intensive after-school floor work to be done upon returning to the library. After a repertoire of books has been built up and the librarian gets used to the pace, it may be possible to do more than two classes.

At the time that you are setting up a schedule for visiting classes in the school, learn the reading level of each class and plan accordingly. Some books are fine for all classes, but you don't want to select difficult adult material for a tenth-grade class reading on a fifth-grade level. Be cautioned, too, that sometimes your feelings about the reading level may vary greatly from those of the teacher. On the advice of the teacher, you may bring a selection of high-low materials, only to discover that the students are not terrible readers after all, but are perfectly average.

In some instances, the teacher may have a specific reference lesson in mind. This can be a delightful experience for both the librarian and the class. However, the librarian should try to persuade the teacher to allow ten to fifteen minutes to talk about some recreational books. The books can be incorporated into the reference lesson. But remember, a reference class that has no real objective, with no finished report at the end, is really a waste of time.

Storytelling can also be done in the school classroom. There are many excellent collections of short stories and folktales that are perfect for this technique. But keep the story short—no more than eight minutes—or it will take up too much of your time. Be careful to select a story that will be of interest to the group: Hero myths and scary ghost stories are particularly effective with teenagers. And if you use a story from a collection that looks obviously childlike, be sure not to bring the book with you.

Discipline

Unlike the library class, where it is possible to have a certain amount of control over the environment, in the school class there is no telling what can happen: The public address system can go on, students can come in late with bathroom passes, or there can be a fire drill or a student government presentation—to name a few possibilities. There is nothing worse than coming to the most dramatic moment of a booktalk and having a fire drill bell go off. But just keep smiling; it's all part of the experience.

It is generally recommended that the class visit be the English classroom rather than the school library. As a visitor, the librarian doesn't want to be a disciplinarian, and the balance that is achieved in a classroom can be easily disturbed when there is a change of environment. Also, bring more materials with you than you can possibly use, so that you can shift your approach depending upon the disciplinary environment in the class. If, for example, the class is not in control, watch the books you select. Don't use joke books or other materials that can set off the students.

Library information

Some libraries have a system that allows students actually to check out books in the classroom. Most, however, make the students come to the library to take out the books. But the students can fill out registration forms for library cards in the classroom for the librarian to take back to the library. For students who have problems with the library, a note can be written on the back of the registration slip addressed to the person in charge of the library branch. Comparing the library card to a charge card brings home to teenagers the importance of not lending their cards and of reporting a lost card.

An effective device is to promise to give a free reserve card to any student in the class if a book that the librarian has spoken about is not in the library when the student comes to borrow it. This helps familiarize the young adults with the reserve or interlibrary loan system. Another nice idea is to have bookmarks or other giveaways for the class. The bookmarks can be related to a theme or just some good books you recommend.

At the end of the class, invite the students to visit you at the public library and tell them that you'll help them with their individual library requests at that time.

The Joy of Booktalking

There is a great deal of work in preparing for booktalk classes. However, the joy that you give and receive cannot be found in any other aspect of library work. When teenagers stop you on the street, in the supermarket, or even in the library itself and tell you how much they enjoyed your visit and how they enjoyed the books, then you know that you have been successful. Each class is an experience, each class is unique. No matter how many classes you do, as soon as you walk in and see those faces smiling up at you, and feel them listening and responding, you will have achieved an important and satisfying personal and professional goal.

III
Information and Referral Services and Networking

10
The Librarian in the Youth Services Network: Nationally and Locally

EVIE WILSON

Some five years ago, youth librarians began attending the national Youth Workers Conferences sponsored by the National Youth Work Alliance. Staff from juvenile justice facilities and nonprofit youth-serving agencies expressed dismay that librarians were attending these conferences. What has the library to do with runaway centers, they asked.

In a time when libraries face a decade of reduced funding, First Amendment confrontations, and elitest and discriminatory computerized information systems, many youth librarians who have provided leadership have done so as a result of the activities of the National Organizations Serving the Young Adult Liaison Committee (NOSYAL) of the Young Adult Services Division (YASD) of the American Library Association (ALA). These are the librarians who take the initiative to go into communities and indicate by example that libraries are indispensable; who provide the leadership for networking services to youth so that agency self-interest can be superseded by more efficient total youth services that do not duplicate or discriminate; who make it plain that information is power.

Interest in forming the NOSYAL committee first began as a result of the work of a parallel committee within the Association for Library Service to Children (ALSC), another ALA division. The NOSYAL committee was established as a YASD standing committee in July 1975. The function statement of both division committees reads the same: "To explore, recommend, initiate, and implement ways of working with other organizations that work with and for young adults [and children, in the case of ALSC]."

YASD determined that there are many national organizations that primarily serve the adolescent age group. A number of these organizations provide programs, conferences, and publications useful to youth librarians. NOSYAL committee members are assigned national organizations with which they are to establish and maintain liaison; all liaisons once documented are approved by the board of directors of YASD as are any special publications or programs resulting from these liaisons. Let's take a look at a few of the resulting projects.

YASD National Liaison Activities

At first, NOSYAL committee members were unsure as to what the most effective method of establishing these liaisons would be—to write letters to national staff or to have a member of a local affiliate of the national organization set up an informal information-sharing meeting. An attempt was made at the outset to assign an organizational caseload to committee members based on their proximity to a particular organization's national headquarters. One of the first youth-serving organizations with which liaison was established was Planned Parenthood Federation of America, whose national offices are in New York City. In nearby Rockland and Westchester counties, New York, the YA librarians had already begun activities with their local Planned Parenthood staff, who subsequently paved the way for further projects on the national level. This liaison, which initially began with exchange of materials and statistics, eventually culminated in the publication of a pamphlet, "Sex Education for Adolescents: A Bibliography of Low-Cost Materials," through the joint efforts of representatives from the Young Adult Services Division, the American Academy of Pediatrics, and Planned Parenthood Federation of America. The pamphlet has been a best-seller for the American Library Association.

The first chair of the NOSYAL committee was Susan Ellsworth, a YA librarian who worked for Prince George's County (Maryland) Hotline. Through her work at this crisis intervention service, in close proximity to the nation's capital, Ellsworth made some contacts with the National Youth Work Alliance. One of the staff there, Tom McCarthy, agreed to be a consultant to the ALA/YASD/NOSYAL committee. The alliance has since offered speakers for YASD programs and conferences, provided consultation in the formation of a legislative network of youth librarians for the purpose of lobbying, and invited youth librarians to be workshop presentors and exhibitors at the annual Youth Workers Conferences. For example, when the conference was held in Seattle, Washington, in June 1981, Susan Madden and Susan Tait (Seattle Public Library) offered a media presentation entitled "Pimples, Puberty, and Passion," which was very popular with conference participants.

The National Network of Runaway and Youth Services, also located in Washington, D.C., has served as a consultant to YASD in various areas of youth advocacy. Brian Dyak, staff member of the network at the time, was the YASD President's Program speaker in June 1979, addressing the topic "The Youth Librarian as Youth Advocate." Dyak had worked closely with the YA consultant of the Tampa-Hillsborough County (Florida) Public Library System in networking youth agencies in that area. This local liaison resulted in the article "Cooperative Grantsmanship: The Young Adult Librarian and Community Networking," which appeared in the Winter 1979 issue of *Top of the News*, a joint publication of ALSC and YASD.

In 1976, YASD/NOSYAL established liaison with the National Commission on Resources for Youth, a national nonprofit organization that encourages youth participation in decision making on both the national and local levels. NCRY acts as a clearinghouse and publication source for youth-participation projects, as well as providing consultation for communities that are seeking to develop such programs and need guidelines for implementation. Prior to 1976, a small but vocal number of youth librarians were already forming youth advisory boards in their libraries to help with book evaluation and to plan and execute library programs for themselves and their peers. Since 1976, valuable assistance has been given to the Young Adult Services Division by National Commission Executive Director Peter Kleinbard and in particular Clearinghouse Coordinator Ellen Lippmann (a former youth librarian).

In 1980, a new YASD committee was formed, Youth Participation in Library Decision-Making. Under chair Jana Varlejs, of Rutgers University, the committee worked closely with committee consultant Ellen Lippmann to develop a position paper, "Guidelines for Youth Participation in Library Decision-Making," (discussed in Chapter 4 of this book and reprinted in Appendix I). The position paper was a significant handout for the YASD President's Program at the 1982 ALA Annual Conference, which featured Eliot Wigginton, editor of the youth-produced Foxfire books. The guidelines are now being developed into a pamphlet, "Youth Participation in Libraries," by the YASD Youth Participation Committee working with the NCRY staff, which also will include program descriptions, suggestions for implementation, and sketches of other library programs. The pamphlet will be published and available nationwide through a grant being sought by both national organizations.

In 1978, Joan Lipsitz, noted authority on the problems and needs of early adolescents, became the director of the Center for Early Adolescence at the University of North Carolina at Chapel Hill. The center acts as a clearinghouse for information, provides speakers and consultants, and publishes monographs and a newsletter. In June 1979, the board of directors of the Young Adult Services Division approved the NOSYAL liaison with the center. Subsequently, youth librarians have worked with the center on several publications, including the center's first monograph, *Understanding Families with Young Adolescents*. Recently, Alice Naylor, chairperson of the Department of Educational Media at Appalachian State University and a member of the Young Adult Services Division, was named a fellow of the Center for Early Adolescence. The center also publishes a newsletter, *Common Focus*. The May/June 1982 issue of this publication, which was entirely devoted to library service to young adolescents, featured articles written by youth-serving librarians from Alabama, Florida, North Carolina, California, Arizona, and Washington. An annotated resources list to aid parents, youth workers, and educators in selecting books and films for young adolescents was included at the end of this issue.

The National Council on Crime and Delinquency (NCCD) has as part of its overall objectives to monitor carefully adjudication and treatment of juvenile delinquents and status offenders. Its Youth Bureau acts as a clearinghouse for alternative youth programs such as runaway centers and halfway houses that serve youthful truants, runaways, dependents, and ungovernables outside of any criminal process. Where there are abuses or lack of adequate funding for programs, the National Council actively advocates correction of these problems. In January 1978, YASD/NOSYAL liaison was established with NCCD. The NOSYAL committee worked with the National Council in identifying advocacy needs for youth in trouble, as well as assisting the council in notifying library review media about the council's film, *The Innocent Criminal.* "Librarians Play New Advocacy Role," written by the chair of the YASD Legislation Committee, appeared in the Spring 1980 issue of *Youth Forum,* NCCD's newsletter.

The NOSYAL committee also maintains liaisons in varying stages of development with the following national youth-serving organizations: Girl Scouts of America, Boy Scouts of America, National Committee for Citizens in Education, Youth Liberation, Boys Clubs of America, Girls Clubs of America, YMCA, YWCA, 4-H Program, SIECUS (Sex Information and Education Council of the U.S.), National Juvenile Law Center, National Council of Teachers of English, AFS International/Intercultural Programs, Child Welfare League of America, Children's Defense Fund, Future Homemakers of America, Junior Achievement, National Center on Institutions and Alternatives, and Salvation Army. Publications of these organizations have been displayed by the NOSYAL committee at ALA annual conferences and at YASD conference programs where appropriate. For further information regarding the activities of this important committee write: Evelyn Shaevel, Executive Director, Young Adult Services Division, American Library Association, 50 East Huron Street, Chicago, IL 60611.

Within the membership of YASD, the impact of the activities of this committee has been considerable. One of the most visible effects has been the expansion of the division's committee structure to reflect the new advocacy component and two new stated objectives of the division (as recorded in the *ALA Handbook of Organization*): (1) to advocate the young adult's right to free and equal access to materials and services and assist librarians in handling problems of such access; and (5) to stimulate and promote the expansion of young adult services among professional associations and agencies at all levels.

At the 1983 midwinter meeting in San Antonio, the YASD board of directors discussed, in an intensive planning session, the expansion of the division's objectives to include yet another objective. The proposed objective would assign certain YASD committees the responsibility of identifying other professional associations with youth interests, such as the American Bar Association. Each organization would then be informed of YASD activities and/or potential contributions that are parallel to the organization's interests and activities.

These objectives and the advocacy and interagency cooperation that they reflect have thus far resulted in the creation of two new division committees: Legislation (standing) and Youth Participation in Library Decision-Making (ad hoc). The Legislation Committee has as its charge:

To serve as a liaison between the ALA Legislation Committee and the division. To inform and instruct librarians working with young adults of pending legislation, particularly that which affects young adults, and to encourage the art of lobbying. To recommend to the YASD Board endorsement or revision of legislation affecting young adults which might be proposed or supported by the ALA Legislation Committee.

The Legislation Committee over the past three years has developed a legislative network of youth librarians who are interested in advocating for youth services—both in and out of libraries.

The cooperative efforts of the NOSYAL, Legislation, and Youth Participation committees have resulted in a number of annual conference programs for the division, which were heavily attended by librarians across the country. The Legislation Committee provided a lobbying program at the 1982 ALA Annual Conference. NOSYAL, working with its parallel committee in the Association of Library Service to Children, held a forum during the New York annual conference at which the staff of other national youth-serving organizations, could inform librarians about their services and publications. This forum is also planned for the annual conference in 1983.

At present, the NOSYAL committee is heavily involved in planning a program with the Center for Early Adolescence for the 1983 conference in Los Angeles. This program will be a small group-type discussion of after-school programs for early adolescents. The center is presenting the program and distributing materials as well.

YASD Local Liaison Activities

Although ALA conference costs are ever increasing, a number of hard-working and enthusiastic youth librarians somehow continue to find the funds to attend YASD conference programs and participate in YASD committee work. As a result of the many effective and even profitable activities of the division's liaisons, the philosophy of many youth librarians concerning the library's role in outreach on the local level has expanded to include specific networking and advocacy activities and publications.

Even before the formation of the Youth Participation Committee, many YA librarians across the country were involving youth in library decision making and program planning. In Leon County, Florida, young adults working with YA librarian Mary Jane Hylton, developed for use with community groups a videotape describing library services. In Tucson, Arizona, young adults plan library programs and publish their own science fiction magazine called *E. T.* (begun before the movie of the same name), with the aid of YA librarian Diane Tuccillo.

Christy Tyson, formerly at Tucson Public, now YA coordinator for Spokane Public Library, assists young adults in publishing the YAAC (Young Adult Advisory Committee) newsletter *Books, Etc.*, which reviews and highlights YA literature and library programs. As a branch librarian in Tampa, Florida, Juanita Pace Suttle worked with young adults in forming the East Gate Branch Puppet Players, who built their own puppet stage and carried puppet shows to local hospitals and other library branches. Suttle, now at Collier Heights Branch of the Atlanta Public Library, is continuing youth involvement in the Atlanta community.

As the news of these various activities spreads through the library world, other librarians who work with youth are inquiring how they can form such youth groups, which help young people make the difficult transition to adulthood by being involved in the decision-making process.

In June 1978, Girls Clubs of America, Inc., held a national conference at the Wingspread Conference Center in Racine, Wisconsin. This conference acted as a national assessment of the needs and problems of young women in the United States and resulted in a publication called *Today's Girls: Tomorrow's Women*, taken from the conference title. Another result of this conference was a series of local conferences, again using the same title.

When the planning stages of a conference began in Tampa, Florida, the YA consultant of the Tampa-Hillsborough County Public Library System was invited to be a member of the conference steering committee. The YA consultant also provided a bibliography and a book exhibit for the conference. At that time, mention was made by Girls Club staff of a similar conference being planned in Seattle, Washington. Knowing the wide variety of YA programs provided by the Seattle Public Library and the advocacy interests of the YA consultant, Susan Madden, information about the Tampa conference as well as a copy of the bibliography were sent to Seattle. This cross-country communication resulted in the publication of the Tampa/Seattle bibliographies, compiled by the two YA consultants, in the 1980 revised edition of *Today's Girls: Tomorrow's Women*. This is an excellent example of the impact that national and local liaisons can have on the total quality of awareness and on information sharing about our nation's young people.

Preparation for Interagency Networking

There is a certain amount of consciousness raising and/or preparation that any youth librarian should execute before making other organizational contacts either nationally or locally. A basic starting point is the pamphlet "Look, Listen, Explain." Produced by a committee of YASD members experienced in outreach services, this publication describes some of the basic ways to assess and analyze local communities and includes forms and checklists that are useful in a step-by-step outreach effort.

A primary prerequisite should be administrative support and approval, which can translate into important financial support in the way of clerical time, probably desk coverage time, and approved professional leave time for interagency meetings and/or ALA conferences. This aspect requires that the youth librarian thoroughly understand and transmit to administration and staff the concept of interagency cooperation as well as background information about the agency or organization with which new activities are to be established.

In order that the librarian be completely ready for "selling" this desired liaison to administration, a complete assessment of the targeted agency should be completed, determining how youth library services can complement the program of that specific organization. Here are some questions that should be determined: What are the overall goals of the organization? Publications? Ages served? Credibility? Funding structure (annual reports are useful sources of such information)? What specific, short-term projects could be developed and completed so that administrators of both organizations will readily perceive the value of continued long-term activities? Who is the staff person who can help facilitate the liaison? Remember that organizations do not respond; people do.

It is important to recognize that although more librarians are taking the library to the community, many youth agencies, especially those offering alternative services, are primarily concerned with crisis intervention and may misunderstand the motives of a youth librarian offering assistance. Many youth-serving agencies in the past have operated under "turf" competitiveness, because financial support coming either from the federal government or from private foundations had to be won through separate agency grant proposals. The idea of a librarian providing the leadership in bringing agencies together for more comprehensive, less duplicating community services will be an unusual one for most community youth workers.

The youth librarian should certainly believe in the appropriateness of providing this leadership. The library, with its variety of resources—print and nonprint—its branches, which reach into all corners of counties and municipalities, and its meeting rooms, is actually the ideal, neutral facility for bringing together organizations of varied services for the purpose of enabling comprehensive services to an age group of constituents that many community organizations are seeking to serve.

Being issue-conscious is also essential for the youth-serving librarian. This means doing some research and being familiar with the major problems and needs of young people, both locally and nationally. This can be easily done—and shared with other agencies—for the librarian has, as a basic resource of his or her profession the indexes and periodicals that compile these problem areas and make them currently available. Knowledge of the issues should be taken into any liaison with another agency. In other words, a youth librarian would not open a liaison meeting with Planned Parenthood of America with a strong antifamily planning statement or a meeting with a runaway facility staff with a plea for incarceration of status offenders in adult facilities. There is a basic need to know the definitions and ramifications of such terms as status offenders, ungovernables, substance abuse, crisis intervention, juvenile justice, at risk, and alternative services. This precaution may seem obvious, but some issues are not so clear-cut and agency relationships may be strained because of ideological conflicts. Therefore, discretion is advisable in the beginning stages.

The pitfall of advertising the library as a "do for" agency should be avoided. Once again, all librarians should first be ethically convinced that information is power and equally convinced of their role in facilitating that power. Thus it should follow that any library staff involved in liaison relationships should be planning *with* not just *for* other organizations. To be assertive in this area may require a certain familiarity with group dynamics as well as program planning and evaluation. These skills have certainly been neglected in courses and workshops in library graduate school curriculums and library continuing education programs. It is as if library educators do not perceive that librarians need basic management and political ability.

Being a mentor is of significant importance for the maintenance of liaison relationships, despite normal library staff promotions and resignations. This means that other members of the library staff also should be encouraged to involve themselves in working with other youth-serving organizations—or at least should be kept informed about these activities so that the organizations involved will have an over-all good feeling about the total library organization.

Positive Results—Future Potential

One of the most positive results of agencies working together is the more thorough dissemination of information across the country right down to the grass-roots level. Not only will parents, youth workers, and librarians be more familiar with community services, but the sharing of information also will facilitate a better understanding of the needs of youth, which will bring about more effective service at all levels. Once again, this may seem to be an obvious benefit. Yet many grass-roots agencies—libraries included—have not yet begun to look beyond the immediate financial needs of their own organizations.

Speaking of financial needs (it is difficult to avoid the topic these days), the types of activities mentioned in this chapter have the potential of increasing cost-effectiveness, nationally and locally. Recently, a national organization serving boys decided to incorporate programs for girls as well. A local staff member recognized that if professionals well versed in the needs of both sexes worked at the outset to plan a joint program of service, it would certainly avoid some duplication of services, especially in smaller communities, which are dependent totally on United Way funding.

Joint fund raising is another potential activity. An existing example of this is the effort now being made by the YASD Youth Participation Committee along with the National Commission on Resources for Youth to identify funding sources for their joint publication on youth participation. With national funds dwindling and what little comes from that source mostly available in block grants, local community foundations and funding sources are urging local organizations to cooperate in grantsmanship efforts whenever possible.

There are many promising areas of common concern, such as joint advocacy for clientele who cannot afford or have limited access to information or services. These potential areas of concern and other activities such as those mentioned in this chapter will have to wait, however, for the library profession to resolve a basic philosophical issue: whether librarians should be primarily custodians of knowledge or whether librarians are under any obligation to take these services (or at least the information about their services) out into the community.

The library profession as a whole gives lip service to community involvement. There may be a great deal of outreach efforts being made by librarians on the grass-roots level, but when the literature is assessed, the number of articles in professional journals highlighting outreach activities seems small compared with library "housekeeping" articles. Only when disasters such as Proposition 13 strike do library professional journals record local political organizing and grass-roots advocacy. Even on the national level, though there may be many informal liaisons between national organizations and ALA's divisions, of the seventy-eight organizations listed in the *ALA Handbook of Organization, 82/83* (pp. 155–156) with which the entire association has liaisons, only thirty-nine of those organizations are outside the strictly education/publishing/information retrieval categories. Most of these thirty-nine liaisons are maintained by ALSC and YASD. Now Priority #2 of the

American Library Association (see *ALA Handbook of Organization, 82/83,* p. 184) reads:

ALA will promote legislation at all levels that will strengthen library and information services. Means will be developed for facilitating the effective competition of libraries for public funds as well as for funds from the private sector.

How can this "facilitation" occur without support from other groups who know, from their own experience, why libraries should receive adequate public funds?

So there remains the question: Is there any relationship between lack of adequate library public relations and outreach, on the one hand, and the increasing lack of support and funding for library services, on the other? Are there available role models of librarians who have successfully developed both organizational and political relationships that have resulted in increased funding? Perhaps librarians should consider that if they cannot reconcile themselves to becoming more aggressive about their image, importance, and budget, then the profession may see many more university librarians conducting fairs and auctions to raise book budget money and many more city/county public library administrators competing with police departments over funding for civil service positions. A large number of youth librarians on the local as well as national level are providing the examples these days for leadership in taking library services to other groups, so that these nightmare scenarios will not play a part in future library administration.

Bibliography

Braverman, Miriam. "Building Grassroots Support for Public Libraries." *Library Journal*, September 15, 1979, pp. 1827–1831.

———. "Does America Need a National Youth Service?" *Educational Record* (Summer 1980): 35–38.

———. "Family Networks and Beyond." *C/O: Journal of Alternative Human Services* 2, no. 2 (July/September 1977): 25–37.

Klepeis, Eleanor F. "A Case Study in Library Cooperation: The King County Youth Service Center." *Library Journal*, April 15, 1973, pp. 1359–1363.

Manley, Will. *Snowballs in the Bookdrop:* Talking It over with Your Library's Community. Hamden, Conn.: Shoe String, 1982. 202 pp. pap.

Ringers, Joseph, Jr. *Creating Interagency Projects.* Community Collaborators, Box 5429, Charlottesville, VA 22903. 1977. 56 pp.

Rothman, Jack H., John L. Erlich, and Joseph G. Teresa. *Promoting Innovation and Change in Organizations and Communities:* A Planning Manual. New York: Wiley, 1976. 309 pp.

Wilson, Evie. "The Young Adult Librarian as Youth Advocate." *Indiana Media Journal* (Winter 1980): 11–13.

Wilson, Evie, and Brian Dyak. "Cooperative Grantsmanship: The Young Adult Librarian and Community Networking." *Top of the News* (Winter 1979): 175–181.

Periodicals

New Designs for Youth Development. Bimonthly. Associates for Youth Development, Box 36748, Tucson, AZ 95740.

Voice of Youth Advocates. Bimonthly. Box 6569, University, AL 35486.

11
Toward Meeting the Information Needs of Young People in New York City

PATRICIA R. ALLEN

Today young people between the ages of six and seventeen make up about 20 percent of New York City's population. More than half of these estimated 1,400,000 youth are black or Hispanic, and of this half there are almost twice as many blacks as Hispanics. Half of those under eighteen live in families with annual incomes of $10,000 or less. At least a third of the children live in single-parent families. A recent survey indicated that several thousand youth were on the streets homeless. The New York City public school system admits that 45 percent of the high school population does not graduate.

These statistics suggest that the information needs of young people go far beyond school assignments, even though libraries continue to be filled after school with teenagers doing their homework. Youth also need information to survive and advance. They need help in finding out what careers and jobs are open to them, help in solving family crises, even help in locating a home or a meal. They need aid in dealing with the consequences of drugs or pregnancy or encounters with the law.

Many of the services they require exist; however, in New York, as in most cities, they are not fully organized or universally accessible. Teens are often unaware of their availability. Given the cuts in school guidance services and community youth programs that have taken place since 1975, services to connect an individual youth with a specific program are lessening.

In New York City, libraries have responded to these needs in a number of ways, including preparing directories. The New York Public Library's Office of Community Services publishes annually the *Directory of Community Services*, covering programs in three of the city's five boroughs. Queens Borough Public Library cosponsored production of *The Queens Book of Youth Programs*, reporting on more than 300 agencies and activities in this borough of nearly two million residents. City libraries also maintain learner's advisory services for teenagers, providing education and employment information and guidance on an individual basis (as discussed in chapter 12 of this book). These substantial efforts, however, are but a fraction of what is needed. One argument of this chapter is that, in the universe of community information services for youth, library resources might most profitably be focused on advancing the advisory function and on taking a more aggressive coordinating stance among existing services than on data collection.

This chapter will describe various efforts underway in New York City to serve the information needs of the city's youth. Although these programs and services exemplify progress to date in many urban areas, they also illustrate what remains to be done. A main thesis here is that to improve community information services for youth, fragmentation of those services must be reduced; this can be achieved through the establishment of both comprehensive and specialized data bases and directories and through the development of a variety of methods to match information to the needs of individual users. Reasons for fragmentation and some strategies for reversing them will be considered. The critical role that both young people and young adult librarians must play in overcoming fragmentation will be discussed.

A Comprehensive Data Bank

Youth need information in a variety of categories, ranging from vocational and career counseling, employment, college preparation, tutoring, health, parenting education, and recreation to emergency shelter, substance abuse treatment and prevention, and legal aid. At the same time, members of their families (whose condition directly affects theirs), may need additional urgent help: homemaker services for an incapacitated parent, relocation for a housing problem, day care for a working parent, marital counseling for parents in difficulty, or aid for a handicapped family member. Ultimately, then, the call is for a basic comprehensive data bank of community services that includes youth resources, not a data bank for youth services only.

In New York City, two current efforts toward this end are underway. In one case, three agencies have come together to create a computerized directory of all social and health agencies in the city. Called the Social Agency Inventory System (SAIS), this project involves the combined efforts of the Community Council of Greater New York, a private coordinating agency; the city government's Human Resource Administration; and the Greater New York Fund/United Way, which is administrative headquarters for the project. As of this writing, some 1,500 agencies with 4,000 service sites have been surveyed and the results fed into a computer. In November 1983, the first directory printed from this data base is scheduled to be published, priced between $30 and $40. Descriptive entries will be listed alphabetically by agency, and an index of 200 taxonomy categories and 140 key words will provide subject access to services. Items are also cross-referenced by client age and geographic location. SAIS is working on plans that would allow agencies or individuals to request specialized printouts and would eventually allow for field terminals. The United Way also maintains its own related information and referral unit.

The United Way has encouraged development of similar computerized data banks throughout the United States. By itself or in connection with local agencies, it is underwriting efforts in several cities and regions, including Fort Lauderdale, Cincinnati, Los Angeles, Miami, Seattle, Chicago, and New York, as well as the entire state of Connecticut and Nassau County, New York State. In Los Angeles and New York City, a government human services unit is a coparticipant.

The second New York City data base is the bilingual *Directory of Community Services*, published annually by the New York Public Library since 1978. In contrast to the SAIS system, coverage is limited to the boroughs of Manhattan, the Bronx, and Staten Island—less than half the city's population. Nevertheless, the latest edition of the *Directory* contains descriptions of 2,200 agencies, providing listings for the many small, community-based groups in these boroughs. In addition, the *Directory* covers a wider range of services, including, for example, a high proportion of educational services. Also, the SAIS system is designed primarily for social workers and others providing information and referral services to social service and health agency clients, whereas the NYPL *Directory* is organized to serve a wider range of constituents. At present, accessibility to current data is much greater through NYPL; when the SAIS system is fully in place, these two projects will represent complementary sources that can be tapped by information seekers.

Matching Youth and Information

With a data base in place, thought turns naturally to its use. This section reviews various ways of individualizing data, that is, of matching specific needs of a young person with the particular services he or she may require. One is by training youth and citizens to serve as data interpreters in specialized topic areas. Another is the more impersonal use of individual profile sheets or workbooks that guide the young person through information processes. Third is the production of specialized directories that focus on resources for youth, and, fourth, issuing mass publications for young people, such as teen newspapers. Note that in many of the following examples youth play a prominent role in the gathering and dissemination of information. Their volunteer involvement can improve both the quality and quantity of information programs and services.

Peer and citizen counseling

"I just received a letter from a former student who graduated from Harvard and has been accepted into Yale Medical School," said Sol Schwartz, head of Project Options at Sheepshead Bay High School in Brooklyn. Schwartz started Project Options in 1975, when he discovered he was the sole college counselor for 2,500 students, most of them from blue-collar, working-class families. Since that time he has trained about fifty young people a year as college information specialists. They help their fellow students select colleges and fill out applications and financial aid forms. Before Project Options, more than 70 percent of the graduating class went on to college, but they selected city and state public universities most of the time. Today the percentage of those attending has risen ten points, and students are attending colleges all over the United States, including Ivy League schools. Naturally, scholarship aid has gone up dramatically.

Health information is available through the Teen Intern Project of Catholic Alternatives, a citywide program that trains young people to share family planning and sexual health information with their counterparts through structured workshops that any youth program can request. A recent session about venereal disease included, for example, an account by a young man of his visit to a venereal disease clinic. By describing step by step what a visitor would encounter from the moment of walking through the door, he demystified the entire process for the group of teenagers who came to the youth center to listen. Counselors go through a thorough thirteen-week training program and a teen hot line provides additional accessibility.

Another program, sponsored by New York City's Maternal Infant Care (MIC), helps parents of ten- to fourteen-year-olds communicate sexual health information. To date, some 150 parents have taken the six-week course. Each participant is sponsored by a community group and is required to conduct workshops for other parents in their neighborhoods. Workshops are held in schools, Head Start classrooms, churches, and community agencies. Parents thus become information sources for their own children and trainers for other parents. Ongoing in-service classes support their training activities.

In its thirteen years of existence, the East Harlem-based Hot Line Cares, started by a teenager who is now the program director, has trained hundreds of young people to perform a variety of information services. The Telephone Crisis Team answers the hot line phones from 10 A.M. to 7 P.M. five days a week. They have fielded thousands of inquiries on topics ranging from the need for a home to emotional and psychological problems. They have helped hundreds of runaways of all ages to find shelter. Teenagers, plus an occasional graduate student, constitute staff.

Their Street Outreach Team takes the hot line into the community. Teen counselors go where young people "hang out," talking with them and recommending appropriate services. And their Angel Dust Team, whose members are aged fifteen to eighteen, have had considerable training in problems related to this dangerous substance, and for several years they have conducted workshops for school classes and community youth groups. They not only lecture but they also do skits, engage in role playing, and encourage questions.

Self-counseling

A vocational project called "My Job Campaign" illustrates how thousands of young people can receive cost-efficient individual help with little or no adult time. "My Job Campaign" is a small booklet produced by Open Doors, a nonprofit agency, in conjunction with the New York City public schools. The back-pocket booklet serves as a self-counseling device, taking the teen user step by step in a log, or diary, form through a job search. Facts about each site where a job interview took place can be recorded, for instance, as well as basic facts needed to complete a job application, such as one's social security number. In short, "My Job Campaign" is a standard outline filled in by the user according to his or her individual case. To date, about 50,000 copies have been printed and distributed to teenagers in New York City. One can imagine similar booklets covering such topics as selecting a high school, defining a potential career area, or upgrading one's health. Single copies of the booklet are available free of charge from Open Doors, 200 Madison Avenue, New York, NY 10016.

Specialized youth directories

Directories that focus on youth services in a specific location or subject can be extremely useful. A variety of such directories have appeared in recent years. In 1978, the New York City's Youth Bureau undertook comprehensive youth planning, encouraged by fiscal incentives from New York State. One major outcome was an invitation from the Youth Bureau to each of the city's fifty-nine neighborhood planning areas, or community boards, to select a youth coordinator who would be paid to operate locally and serve the district's population, ranging from 150,000 and 250,000. Currently all but a handful of community boards have such coordinators. Each coordinator has undertaken a survey of youth resources and service needs, and many have prepared some type of district youth directory. This grass-roots service identification has not yet been fed systematically into the major data banks and back again, but the potential is definitely there.

The Citizens Committee for New York City produced two

youth directories between 1979 and 1981; this author served as editor for both projects. *Youthbook* describes more than 250 model and key youth services in the city. Designed as a program idea source more than a comprehensive directory, it describes a wide range of programs drawn from all over the city.

Youth played an important role in the production of *Youthbook*. A number of high school interns prepared entries, and a few students volunteered considerable administrative time. As part of its preparation, a group of junior high schoolers were trained in observation methods. They spent several weeks visiting a large number of the programs and completing observation forms. Transportation was paid for. The students filled out a form for each visit, commenting on their impression of services and securing certain facts about the site not easily available over the telephone. Their comments were taken seriously, and in some cases resulted in programs being added or deleted from the book. Several times the inspectors themselves derived benefit from their program of the day; furthermore, they indicated in several cases that they were recommending the service to family or friends. As one weary teenager commented on her return from a trip to the far reaches of Brooklyn, "It tooks us an hour and a half to get there, but it was worth it!"

Youthbook can be ordered for $3 plus $1.50 postage from Citizens Committee for New York City, 3 West 29 Street, New York, NY 10001.

The Citizens Committee joined forces with the Queens Borough Public Library to produce in 1981 the most thorough youth directory for one borough ever published, *The Queens Book of Youth Programs*. The work includes more than 300 entries about health, art, education, family service, recreation, legal, career, handicapped, youth participation, and multiservice programs. Editorial work was done by the Citizens Committee, and the library helped with research and printed the edition of 2,000 copies, distributed free of charge within six months.

Youth made major contributions to *Queens Book*. A high school senior was coeditor, researching and writing on some fifty agencies. Several other student interns prepared articles and received credit in the acknowledgments. A high school student designed the cover and inserted headlines and graphics throughout the book

It is estimated that to report on the entire city in this fashion would require eight additional volumes—two each for

Brooklyn, Manhattan, and the Bronx, one for Staten Island, and one for citywide programs—each costing about $40,000, including printing.

Directories on special topics include that issued in 1981 by the New York City public schools. It lists more than 200 community-based tutoring programs for students in grades 1 through 9. The schools printed 25,000 newsprint copies and distributed them throughout the city, mainly to 18,000 students in jeopardy of being held back a grade under a new promotional policy. Also, the Manhattan Junior League prepared a guide to resources for learning-disabled children, and a special education training unit of the schools issued a citywide guide to special education programs and services.

Many other directories are still needed. For example, a recent study of the city's Juvenile Probation Department found that the main source of referral information used by 200 juvenile probation officers was a directory more than four years old.

Citywide teen newspapers

Perhaps the hardest part of meeting youth information needs is getting the word to young adults that services really exist. New York is fortunate to have an outstanding monthly newspaper produced by teenagers for teenagers, just finishing its third year of operation.

Recent issues of *New Youth Connections* (*NYC*) have included special resource lists for suicide prevention, legal services, pregnancy tests, and sex counseling. Information on careers, recreation, finances, employment, and health appears frequently. The paper, which costs about $120,000 a year to produce, anticipates it will be 50 percent self-supporting through advertising in a reasonable time. Surveys show that 250,000 teens read each of the 60,000 monthly issues of *NYC*, making it undoubtedly the largest single source of current information for young people in New York City. Each month staff drops off bundles at more than 150 schools and agencies around the city, free of charge. The three New York City library systems distribute copies to approximately 200 branch sites. Single copies are also mailed out to subscribers.

NYC is one of several citywide student newspapers started by the Robert F. Kennedy Memorial Foundation in Washington, D.C., a national youth policy and youth information organization. Others are *The Eye*, in Delaware, and *New Ex-*

pression, in Chicago. In each case a cadre of young people drawn from area high schools constitute staff and an editorial board that makes decisions about newspaper content.

To obtain a sample copy of *New Youth Connections,* write 29 West 21 Street, New York, NY 10010. For a copy of *The Eye,* write Youth Communications/Delaware, Box 1148, Wilmington, DE 19899; and for *New Expression,* contact Youth Communications/Chicago, 207 South Wabash, Chicago, IL 60604.

Reducing Fragmentation

The current youth information picture in New York City is not completely bleak. Comprehensive data bases, varied ways of matching information with people's needs, and some intermediate guidance tools are essential; and there is no question that New York City has made some headway with these matters. However, additional steps need to be taken to reduce confusion and fragmentation of information about existing services.

Networks of people

New Youth Connections does bring the teenage community together, but no comparable publication or organization does the same for youth workers and adults concerned about young people. Only the Bronx has a genuine boroughwide youth service organization: the Bronx Council for the Advocacy of Children and Youth (BCACY). Organized in the mid-1970s, the council now has more than 200 individual and agency members, organized into task forces on such topics as child abuse, education, and mental health. The group influenced human service practices in its borough and in the state. And when people know each other, they can talk with each other, offer support, and cut through red tape.

The absence of additional borough structures and a citywide counterpart represents a serious shortcoming in New York City. There is also no organized training program or joint problem-solving organization for youth workers. The extent of human connections and the sharing of information among youth workers definitely affect, in turn, the information available to young people.

In a city like New York, many specialized lists and directories of services for young people and their families are needed, and many agencies and individuals have the information and practical ability to produce them. It is almost impossible, however, to keep track of projects in progress. Foundations and corporations that are approached for publication funds do consult with each other, bringing a little order to the scene. In times of limited funds and considerable fragmentation, there would be merit in having a quasi-independent youth and family publications coordination unit for the city. Including writing, editing, and graphics staff, such a unit could assist groups to produce a listing or directory and/or produce its own. It could train adults and youth in editing, information gathering, and publication techniques, and it could lobby for publishing resources and advise on a wide range of services about the kinds of information and publications most needed. At the very least, the unit could serve as an idea clearinghouse for those wishing to publish, thus avoiding duplication of effort. Lack of such coordination remains a gap in the service system.

A central intelligence

Not only publications need to be coordinated. In the ideal (and nonpolitical) world, there would be an overall coordinating unit to make sense out of the universe of programs and promote activities that bring young people to answers they need; to sight information service gaps and bring together forces to fill them. However, information is power and, hence, political. Whether so much power should be concentrated in one place is a difficult question. It might even be that some division of activity is wise.

So lack of coordination, then, is a mixed blessing. What seems reasonable, however, is some broad coordination around topic areas. In New York, the Community Council has convened various task forces around service areas such as recreation. Thus the city's Parks Department representatives do talk with staff from the Boy Scouts and Girl Scouts, the Police Athletic League, and other major recreation service providers. The work of this task force did, for example, change the city policy on opening schools after hours for recreation.

There is another political aspect that should not be ignored. Knowing that children under eighteen do not vote, many elected officials are not unhappy that this constituency is fragmented. They can be less than enthusiastic about efforts to improve coordination. One could even argue that money is not forthcoming in large amounts for community information services for this very reason. Those who care about such matters must be inventive in circumventing such obstacles.

Yet another political consideration is "turf." The public schools found tutoring programs everywhere: in churches, in after-school school programs, in community groups. Schools and nonprofit community agencies must struggle to communicate, and cooperate. Even units within a bureaucracy find it hard to speak with each other. There is an interagency council for the aging in New York City government, but nothing comparable among the seventeen or so city government units that serve young people in some way. As in most cities, we can be grateful for the promise, but must work to achieve it and be willing to cooperate once communication lines are established.

A Role for Young People and Librarians

Those who believe in youth participation as a way of enriching a program and advancing youth development are quick to say that young people should have a real voice in information matters. At present, however, there is no citywide information policy, or youth information policy, that defines a role for youth or adults in its making or execution. No one is creating a citywide Youth Information Corps that would train young people as community information specialists.

Nevertheless, librarians and information specialists can help youth play a role now. In particular, they can help young people gain training in questioning and information skills.

In urban areas youth face information handicaps. An information source may practice prejudice and refuse to provide a young person with information. Poor reading ability or English-speaking skills may hamper the search. Many young people do not know how to ask questions effectively, and many cannot write a letter of inquiry. Although the New York City public schools have recently added an office of critical thinking and reasoning, and the Vermont Department of Education has even declared that reasoning is a basic competency to be addressed in the curriculum, the impact of this new priority has not yet hit most classrooms.

Librarians can assist in developing these capabilities through large-scale training courses affecting new teachers, citizens, and youth—those willing, in turn, to teach others. Lack of these skills will hamper youth's reception and use of information.

Librarians are also specialists with immense skill in identifying and providing information for youth. They can locate projects that are trying to do this and provide any aid that is feasible. For example, in their immediate community there might be various information and referral programs, a peer counseling project, or a job placement service. It is entirely appropriate for librarians to bring together representatives from these organizations to facilitate communication and coordination of services.

Librarians need to pull together those with a vision of how young people can take part in making some order from the mass of information they encounter on the streets, from the schools, from television, from their families. Those who see youth as capable of acting on their own, and feel it is important for them to be independent and competent, need to offer youth support in personal and practical ways. For there are many not willing to surrender adult autonomy and perfectionism to imperfect youth so that they can have the experience of finding out for themselves. In many respects, defining an active role for youth represents the first step in developing an active information system for young people.

12
Learner's Advisory Services for Young Adults

EMMA COHN

There is very little that the educational system can do directly to create new jobs. Rather its role is a supportive one that stresses the development of skills required by business and industry. In this process educators must reach out to business leaders in the business market area, especially at the local level, to establish connections between school districts, colleges, universities and community-based organizations and the business community. . . .

As a first alternative the Regents support the establishment of multi-service centers as a response to the need for greater coordination of services at the local level. . . . Funds would be used not to duplicate existing services but to provide initial points of access for most-in-need youth requiring information about local employment opportunities, access to education and training programs, and the provision of human services within a community. . . .

—Youth Education and Employment:
A Comprehensive Approach (Policy
statement by the Board of Regents,
April 1982, The University of the State
of New York, the State Education Department, Albany, NY 12234)

When I first began to work in the public library, reference work disappointed me. It seemed to be related more to materials than to people. I decided to become a young adult librarian because services to teenagers were more actively involved with the cultural growth of the individual and with schools and other community agencies. Young adult librarians have a strong belief in their role as educators who serve the needs of the teenage community outside of and beyond the formal classroom setting. The recent development of the Learner's Advisory Service (LAS) is an excellent example.

LAS, which began in 1975 as a career and guidance service for adults, was sponsored by the Adult Independent Learning Project within the College Entrance Examination Board (CEEB), headed by Jose Orlando Toro, a dynamic and creative educator who is also a librarian. Funded by the Council on Library Resources, the National Endowment for the Humanities, and the U.S. Office of Education, as well as by CEEB, training by a national faculty drawn from the library, education, and social science professions was provided to the staff of participating libraries: the statewide library network of New York, Atlanta Public Library, Denver Public Library, Enoch Pratt Free Library (Baltimore), Miami-Dade Public Library (Florida), Portland (Maine) Public Library, Salt Lake City Public Library, St. Louis Public Library, Tulsa City-County Public Library, and the Free Library of Woodbridge (New Jersey).

In New York, a transfer training concept was used. The national faculty conducted seminars for a team of librarians representing each library system within the network, and the teams in turn trained librarians in their respective systems. The training included program planning and evaluation, psychology of the adult learner, educational planning and decision making, interviewing, and the selection and use of study materials. The national office assisted the librarians with the testing and evaluation of the service and provided the initial publicity materials. Each library, within the context of its own strengths and community resources, planned and tested services to help adults learn on their own.

The Nathan Straus Young
Adult Library

In 1978, at the urging of The New York Public Library's Office of Young Adult Services, a Learner's Advisory Service was begun on a half-time basis in the Nathan Straus Young Adult

Library, a demonstration center for work with teenagers that is located in the Donnell Library Center in Manhattan. For about three years, the specially trained adult librarians who had begun the LAS helped all who came, young people as well as adults—but especially teenagers between the ages of thirteen and eighteen—to find educational programs, vocational training, and all kinds of community resources.

A young adult librarian trained by New York Public Library LAS staff was appointed to develop and operate the service at Nathan Straus. The main purpose of the service is to have materials available for any learning project that a teenager might undertake. Of equal importance are the in-depth interviews between the student and the young adult librarian, during which they explore all of the educational possibilities available for the young adult.

The collection began with handbooks, directories, guides, information sources, and catalogs from colleges and technical and specialized schools. Material was also gathered on financial aid to young people, tests and testing, the high school equivalency diploma, and local New York City community services. A concerted effort was made to have the new LAS placed on all appropriate educational mailing lists. Circulating books of special interest to teenagers, both fiction and nonfiction, were added to the collection, as was a vertical file on careers.

Although students are welcome to drop in, the Learner's Advisory Service generally makes appointments with the young clients in advance. The student is interviewed to determine individual problems, needs, and goals. Most learners need advice and referral; some actually need counseling and help in making decisions. The telephone can be enormously helpful—especially in making a first contact with an admissions office or a city agency, which is often difficult for a young person to do on his or her own. The librarian's role varies with the young person's need. As Louise Spain, the first LAS young adult librarian, wrote in an annual report:

One of my first clients was a 19-year old who was currently enrolled in a high-school equivalency course. He returned for a discussion of college and careers after he passed the test and revisited the center many more times to report on his progress and say hello. Several foreign-born young people appeared, looking for English as a Second Language courses, and infor-

mation on how to evaluate their foreign credentials for college admission. I was momentarily taken aback when one Chinese eighth grader asked for courses in Mandarin Chinese and Latin—the former was easier to find. Several high school juniors confided their plans to enter Yale, Princeton, or Harvard Medical School. These few were usually very well informed, but wanted to know about summer jobs, vocational testing or SAT preparation sources. Several families came in with a teenager in tow: one wanted an automotive high school program for their son who had recently arrived from Canada. The local Board of Education had failed to inform them about the alternative high school programs which provided this training. Another family was concerned that their Italian-born son find a good summer course to improve his English. Still another was dragged in by her sister. She told me almost belligerently that she hated school and tests and liked to work with her hands. When I suggested apprenticeship training, they eagerly took down all the information and left happily.

Although many requests are similar, each person is unique, Spain points out. Several students may want math or reading tutoring, but one wants it close to home and another will travel, apparently in an effort to avoid going home. One needs tutoring in order to get ready for college, another needs help in passing high school algebra. Some young people, when filling out the short printed form, make it clear that they are interested in *everything*—for example, "animals, modeling, chess, and track," or "music, ceramics, and video workshop," or "science, calligraphy, career exploration, and improvement of reading and homework" or "electronics, music, astrology, anthropology, and archaeology." Even when they write only "choosing a college," it is not unusual to find out during the interview that they are also interested in financial aid and, perhaps, in some remedial courses as well.

For those who wonder about the actual length of the interviews, Spain says:

Many of my interviews lasted an hour or more at first, as I listened, searched for information, made calls, provided as many possibilities and covered as many areas as seemed necessary. More people are now making appointments, and the time involved is more likely to be thirty to forty-five minutes each.

The location of this first Learner's Advisory Service for teenagers, within the Nathan Straus Library, made it possible to introduce the new career and guidance service to school classes, usually eighth grade through high school, coming to the library to hear booktalks. When nonschool groups from the Police Athletic League and Phoenix House, a drug rehabilitation center, were referred to the Nathan Straus Library by various libraries in the New York metropolitan area, and others came through a flier that had been mailed to them about the Nathan Straus summer youth programs, they, too, were told about the library's special career and vocational services.

In time, the LAS began to get its own requests for group visits. The momentum increased until 1980, when the Community Council of Greater New York brought in seventeen classes, altogether 170 students aged sixteen to nineteen, who were working part time, were going to high school part time, or were involved in counseling several hours per week. Their job developer arranged to have them visit various institutions and work places to broaden their horizons. Now it is hoped that all of the young adult librarians in The New York Public Library system will become aware of what the LAS has to offer teenagers and how they can participate in broadening the scope of its work.

Staten Island's New Dorp Branch Library

An outstanding example of cooperation now exists between Staten Island's New Dorp Branch Library and an organization called the Staten Island Continuum of Education. The Continuum's program to help the public and private high schools of Staten Island with a computerized college guidance system is funded through a grant from the U.S. Department of Education and a combination of other public and private funds. Hooked into a national information center developed at Dartmouth College in New Hampshire, the Continuum serves the high schools on a rotating schedule with terminals and equipment, which it owns, and also provides a guidance counselor to work with the students during the week.

When the Continuum's director read in the local newspaper that the New Dorp Branch Library might have to eliminate its pilot Learner's Advisory Service project because of lack of funding, she offered to lend the Continuum's equipment to New Dorp on Saturday afternoons when it was not being used in the schools. The guidance counselor would also be available to work with the public library's young adult specialist. The only elements that The New York Public Library had to supply were the all-important extra telephone line in the branch and space for the equipment.

The college information that young people receive (on a printout that they can take home to their parents) is very specific. For example, the computer will indicate exactly where a student can study pediatric nursing on the west coast of the United States, or which college with a student population of under 1,000 is coeducational and Methodist.

In the area of guidance, the computer asks the students questions about their career goals and offers career suggestions on the basis of their answers. This is where the human element comes in. Sometimes the computer does *not* suggest the career in which the student is most interested. It is the guidance counselor and the librarian who can tell the student why. One girl was interested in forensic science — the science of criminal pathology — but her career test indicated that she lacked aptitudes for many of the career's requirements. To help understand her limitations, the librarian found some books on forensic science. It quickly became apparent from these sources that the student would first have to go into the field of medicine before she could go into forensic science.

Although staff shortages and funding cuts within The New York Public Library during the past three years make the expansion of new services difficult, the LAS engenders such enthusiasm among the staff and public alike that anyone who has become involved with it feels certain that it will continue to grow and will flourish. Part-time staffing arrangements can be successful. When service is by appointment, even twelve to sixteen hours per week can be significant in a large branch or borough center. Of course, there is a considerable investment of training time by the LAS supervisor, but in New York this is done with enthusiasm, particularly in connection with the ROAR program (Return of Active Retirees).

An experienced former young adult librarian working in the LAS in the Bronx (New York) center reports that twelve hours per week can be effective, if the desk is open four hours per day on three afternoons—Saturday being one of the afternoons. This desk, partially screened by bulletin boards, is located in the reference area, and the reference staff takes appointments for the LAS when the part-time librarian (the retiree) is not there. All ages are served, but out of forty people who made appointments in the past three months, seventeen were "under twenty-one." Among the first to come were three of the pages on the staff, during their breaks and lunch hours. Ivette is interested in fashion, and Shawn and Frances in accounting. They have explored vertical files, college catalogs, and career books as they look into their chosen fields. Best of all they have steered numerous other young people to the LAS desk during its open hours.

The young veterans who spent a couple of years in the U.S. Army right out of high school are some of the most serious young learners. With their formerly provincial outlooks considerably broadened after they have been away from home, they have a new appreciation of the city and its educational resources. One young man, interested somewhat vaguely in health careers, did not know exactly what he wanted. When he found a book on holistic health in the LAS collection, he was completely enthralled. The book described the spiritual dimension of health and healing that exactly described the feelings that he had never been able to articulate. But in searching through curricula offered in accredited colleges, neither he nor the librarian could find precisely what he was looking for. What he learned was that he would have to enter the health services in some known area, such as physical therapy or occupational therapy, and then go on to develop in his own way.

Helping adults who are involved with young people is another important aspect of the Learner's Advisory Service. A young woman drafting a proposal to the National Endowment for the Humanities found that the information about community groups in the Bronx was exactly what she needed to know in order to reach the teenagers who would become members of her filmmaking workshops.

Learner's Advisory Service can and should become a part of the training of every young adult librarian. A core collection of materials (such as those listed in the following bibliography) can be formed in almost any size branch and if proper referral can be realized within a system, the satisfactions to both young reader and librarian will be bright and rewarding.

Materials for Young Adults on Education and Employment Opportunities*

Books

COLLEGE SELECTION GUIDES

Each of several guides to the colleges has different strengths. Good first choices with fairly complete and up-to-date information include the following:

The College Handbook 1982–83. 20th ed. New York: The College Board, 1982. $12.95 pap. A descriptive guide to about 3,000 colleges, universities, junior colleges, and technical institutes. Information includes curriculum, admissions requirements, student life, annual expenses, and data on financial aid.

Index of Majors, 1982–83. 5th ed. New York: The College Board, 1982. $10.95 pap. Major programs of study at more than 2,400 two-year and four-year colleges. Includes lists of colleges that have religious affiliations, study abroad programs, cooperative education (work/study programs), independent study, and special admissions.

The following guides supplement the above:

Barron's Profiles of American Colleges: Descriptions of the Colleges. Vol. I. rev. ed. New York: College Division for Barron's Educational Series, 1982. $10.95 pap. Contains a "College Admissions Selector" useful for gauging the level of selectivity of each college, from most competitive to noncompetitive.

James Cass and Max Birnbaum. *Comparative Guide to American Colleges.* 10th ed. New York: Harper & Row, 1981. $11 pap. This also includes a selectivity index and a religious affiliation index, but more notably, an index by major subjects, which lists institutions in order of the number of baccalaureate degrees conferred in that subject (for example; Indiana University at Bloomington conferred the largest number of degrees, 16, in African languages).

Michael Edelhart. *College Knowledge.* New York: Doubleday Anchor Books, 1979. $10.95 pap. Subtitled "Everything you need to know about everything: roommates, shelter, money, jobs, parents, tests, studying, financial aid, travel." Written in a chatty, personal style by a young college graduate in his twenties. Good information and

*Prepared by The Learner's Advisory Service Staff of The New York Public Library, Branch Libraries.

recommendations for further reading; wide-ranging guide to living on one's own in a college environment.

Karen C. Hegener, editor. *National College Databank*. 2nd ed. Princeton, N.J.: Peterson's Guides, 1981. $8.95 pap. An index to colleges grouped according to their unusual characteristics such as colleges that forbid alcohol on campus, or those that accept 50 percent or more of their applicants, or those with athletic scholarships.

The Insider's Guide to the Colleges. Compiled and edited by the staff of the Yale Daily News. New York: Berkley, 1982. $9.95 pap. "Written by students for students—what the colleges are really like."

Frank C. Leana. *Getting into College*. New York: Hill & Wang, 1980. $11.95. An inside look at college applications and admissions. What to look for when choosing a college, the college visit and interview, the personal essay, the importance of test scores, admissions options, recommendations, financial aid, and the role parents play.

Thomas C. Hayden. *Handbook for College Admissions*. New York: Atheneum, 1981. $7.95 pap. Subtitled "A high school student's guide to understanding the college admissions systems." Written by a director of college placement, this includes the application, the interview, financial aid, test scores, and a section called "Making the Most of the Freshman Year."

Fred Zuker and Karen C. Hegener. *Peterson's Guide to College Admissions*, 1983. 3rd ed. Princeton, N.J.: Peterson's Guides. $9.95 pap. Written by an admissions officer and a college guide specialist, this book has a step-by-step coverage of the entire admissions process, including information on financial aid, choosing a college, and preparing for SATs.

ALTERNATIVES TO COLLEGE

John Bear, Ph.D. *The Alternative Guide to College Degrees and Non-Traditional Higher Education*. New York: Putnam's, 1980. $6.95. A good survey of nontraditional college programs, including schools with no required residency and no required courses, schools requiring a very short time on campus, weekend and summer programs, experimental schools, CLEP (college level examination programs), correspondence courses, and external degrees. This has good information about nontraditional graduate programs, therefore less pertinent for use by young adults, but is exceptionally valuable for its evaluation of some of these unusual programs, and warnings against degree mills, diploma mills, and schools of questionable repute.

STUDY GUIDES FOR TAKING TESTS

Murray Shapiro et al. *Barron's How to Prepare for the ACT-American College Testing Program*. 3rd ed. Woodbury, N.Y.: Barron's, 1980. $6.95 pap.

Gabriel P. Freedman et al. *Scholastic Aptitude Test. SAT.* New York: Arco, 1980. $6.95 pap.

Jacqueline Robinson, ed. *Complete Preparation for High School Entrance Examinations.* New York: Arco, 1981. $6.95 pap.

Clif Jenkins et al. *How to Prepare for the New High School Equivalency Examination (C.E.D.)* New York: McGraw-Hill, 1978. $5.95 pap. These question-and-answer workbooks cover a wide range of teenage requests for test preparation, from entrance into specialized high schools, to Scholastic Aptitude Tests, to High School Equivalency tests. Another useful tool in this area is the Protape College Entrance Examination Review Course, which consists of two workbooks and six audiocassettes in the math and verbal parts of the SATs.

FINANCIAL AID FOR EDUCATION

Scholarships, Fellowships, Grants and Loans. The College Blue Book. 18th ed. New York: Macmillan, 1981. $40. Listings in area studies, environmental studies, humanities, life-medical-physical and social sciences, minorities, and technology.

Oreon Keeslar. *Financial Aids for Higher Education, 1982–83.* 10th ed. Dubuque, Iowa: William C. Brown, 1982. $17.95 pap. A comprehensive guide to information about financial aid and a listing of programs. The index can pinpoint programs for children of veterans or particular minorities or nationalities. Also aid from church groups, youth clubs, labor unions, or corporations. Special talents or careers are also indexed.

College Cost Book, 1982–83. 3rd ed. New York: The College Board, 1982. $9.95 pap. Not only does this give a broad overview of the college admission and financial aid process but it also contains The College Board's annual survey, "Student Expenses at Postsecondary Institutions," with over 3,200 schools and colleges listed.

Gail Ann Schlacter. *Director of Financial Aids for Women 1982.* 2nd ed. Santa Barbara, Calif.: ABC-Clio. $26 text ed. A listing of scholarships, fellowships, loans, grants, internships, awards, and prizes designed primarily or exclusively for women; women's credit unions; sources of state educational benefits; and reference sources on financial aids.

CAREER AND VOCATIONAL GUIDANCE

Occupational Outlook Handbook, 1982–83. U.S. Department of Labor, Bureau of Labor Statistics. This is a primary source for brief descriptions of most occupations, including places of employment, training and qualifications, earnings and working conditions, places to write for additional information, and most importantly, the employment outlook for each occupation in the 1980s.

Richard Nelson Bolles. *What Color Is Your Parachute?* Berkeley, Calif.: Ten Speed Press, 1983. $7.95 pap. "A book with practical step-by-step instructions for you, based on the most creative, practical method of job-hunting known in the world today" says the preface. Using exercises and charts, it helps the job hunter or career changer to identify skills and interests in selecting a job and the steps to take to find it.

J. T. Biegeleisen. *Job Resumes.* New York: Putnam's. $4.95 pap. This includes a useful portfolio of sample resumes, from architect to scientist, with one for part-time employment that would be helpful for teenagers. For a free "give-away" on the same subject, the New York State Department of Labor publishes "Guide to Preparing a Resume," available from the Office of Public Information.

William N. Yeomans. *Jobs 82–83. Where They Are—How to Get Them.* New York: Putnam's, 1982. $6.95 pap. For college students and graduates who want projections for employment in the 1980s and suggestions for career choice based on major. Yeomans suggests the jobs to look at first for a particular major. A directory describes each field and its employment outlook.

Bernard Haldane. *Job Power: The Young People Job Finding Guide.* Washington, D.C.: Acropolis, 1980. $10.95, $4.95 pap. Written especially for young people but with methods that can work for anyone. Professional counselor Bernard Haldane presents his system to uncover your best skills and talents, ways to beat the "no experience" syndrome and to secure all the contacts you need.

Kirby W. Stanat with Patrick Reardon. *Job Hunting Secrets and Tactics.* Piscataway, N.J.: New Century, 1977. $5.95 pap. Job hunting again: using the agencies, preparing for the interview, researching the organization, selling the recruiter.

Filmstrips

Me and Jobs. No. 321. New York: Educational Design, 1979.
1. What do I have that a job needs?
2. The job environment and me
3. Want ads
4. Application forms, job interview skills

Financing Education Beyond High School. Washington, D.C.: Student Financial Assistance Training Program, 1979. Explanation of the opportunities for financial assistance.

Films

Anything You Want to Be. 25 min. American Telegraph and Telephone. Men in jobs traditionally reserved for women, and vice versa.

Code Blue. About 35 min. National Audiovisual Center. Hospital and medical jobs and an exhortation to minority groups to help serve their people by entering the health field.

Get a Job. About 12 min. Wind-True Productions. Humorous enactments of the job interview situation, showing obvious do's and don'ts.

Interview: Ready or Not. 24 min. Churchill Films. Brings out the most effective way to prepare for a job interview through self-evaluation and becoming able to project one's strengths to the interviewer.

Other Women, Other Work. 20 min. Churchill Films. Women working in traditionally male fields, such as truck driver, roof shingler, pilot, carpenter.

Where Do I Fit In? 15 min. Manpower Education Institute of America. How teenagers should act on their first job.

Women in Communications. 15 min. BFA Educational Media. Working as cinematographer, reporter, disc jockey.

13
Library Resource Sharing for Youth: The INTERSHARE Network

JOAN NEUMANN

Right alongside "liberty and justice for all" is the ideal articulated for us by the National Commission on Libraries and Information Science:

To eventually provide every individual in the United States with equal opportunity of access to that part of the total information resource which will satisfy the individual's educational, working, cultural and leisure-time needs and interests, regardless of the individual's location, social or physical condition or level of intellectual achievement.[1]

In the state I know best, the New York State Education Department rephrases the same goal:

Regents policy on libraries affirms that every resident of New York State should enjoy timely and free access, through local libraries working within library systems, to a full range of informational resources and services, provided without restriction of censorship or violation of privacy. "Free access" means access without regard to the age, sex, cultural or ethnic back-ground, or other personal characteristics of the user.[2]

Naturally, one expects reality to fall well short of the ideal. But are we serious about extending access to information to young people—no matter who owns it, where it is, and in what form? In practice, only the institutionalized seem to be more systematically excluded from shared resources. In New York, for example, despite the policy quoted above, and four years of pilot sharing through school library systems, the New York State Inter-Library Loan (NYSILL) Network manual still states under "Who May Use NYSILL": "Only two categories are spe-cifically excluded from referral beyond the State Library in the NYSILL Network: persons under 18 years of age and inmates of mental or penal institutions."[3] And under "What Materials May Not Be Requested," the manual declares: "Requests for children's books are not eligible for referral unless accom-panied by a statement indicating a specific and serious research need."[4]

I have been assured that the age restriction may be over-looked if the request is adult enough, but the state library does not collect children's materials and there is no contract with any referral library to provide such resources.

Experiment in Access

I am pointing a finger at New York only for delay in imple-menting consistent change. New York must be praised for will-ingness to experiment with methods that draw school libraries into systems and link these new school library systems into regional intersystem cooperative networks with all other types of libraries.

Twelve pilot school library systems in big cities have been funded since 1979 to help them develop a systematic way of sharing library resources and services with the Bureau of Co-operative Educational Services (BOCES). Two pilot regional intersystem cooperative networks were similarly established to connect all types of libraries in the region. These pilots were expected to run for four years, through June 30, 1983.

The INTERSHARE regional network pilot project, for which I began as project coordinator and became director, is made up of three of the school library system pilots, four public library systems, and the reference and research library system of the region. The highly urbanized metropolitan area that INTER-SHARE serves (New York City and Westchester County) includes almost half the population of the State.

INTERSHARE and RARE, the network pilot in the Rochester region, were chosen competitively from applications from the nine regions of the state to test a broader level of resource sharing. INTERSHARE's program emphasizes (1) the facilitation of interlibrary loan among libraries of all types in the region and the improvement of access to NYSILL for materials not available within the region; (2) the improvement of reference services to library users through their own libraries and the extension of these services when libraries are closed; and (3) assistance to school library systems so they can participate fully in resource sharing.

In order to foster resource sharing among schools and with other types of libraries within the region, school library systems had to establish means to locate library materials within school libraries and provide interlibrary loan, delivery, and consultant services. Although each of the twelve school library system pilots in the state, including each of the three in the INTERSHARE region, is unique, the state has developed a composite of a typical school library system from pilot reports:

This imaginary school library system is BOCES-based and has two full-time persons on the staff who are paid from grant funds. They include a certified school librarian with the title project coordinator and a clerical assistant. The "typical" school library system serves 53 schools with a total enrollment of 35,000; among these are four non-public schools with 1,400 students. The system's schools have 2,400 teachers and administrators.

The principal administrator is a project director who is the BOCES educational communications director and whose salary is paid from BOCES funds. The project director spends approximately ten percent of working time on the pilot project. BOCES administrative and support staff (particularly those in delivery service operations) are important supplements to the school library system. The system is assisted by a twelve-member advisory council which includes school librarians, teachers and administrators, a public librarian, and a student.

Both the project coordinator and the project director

generally meet with the advisory committee. The project coordinator's work includes: program and policy development, supervision of staff, consultation and training of staff of member schools, and communication with the members, with the regional network (if the pilot is part of RARE or INTER-SHARE), and with the State Education Department.

The "typical system" has developed a computerized union catalog with information about 42,000 books and 500 periodical titles located in 53 member schools. As a member of a regional network, the system has access to other catalogs in the region for use in interlibrary loan. In 1981–82, member libraries used the system to borrow 2,700 items; most (80 percent) came from other school libraries in the system. Public libraries supplied about ten percent of the loans. About ten percent of the loans were in the form of photocopy or microfiche.

The "typical system" used the BOCES delivery system for interlibrary loan and for transporting other materials. The delivery truck made weekly stops at 45 delivery/pickup points.

In 1981–82, the system provided 23 seminars and workshops which 380 librarians and teachers attended. During 22 visits and 43 telephone calls to member libraries, the project coordinator provided consultant services, discussed services, and resolved problems. The system published nine bibliographies and reading kits. The system issued four issues of a newsletter which described services and provided information of importance to member libraries.[5]

The Sharing Community

The school library systems being piloted in New York State have been called third-generation library systems. These school library systems join the first generation of public library systems organized more than thirty years ago in the state. The first-generation systems have developed a wide range of technical and consultant support services for member libraries that include union catalog development and interlibrary loan.

In addition, there are the second-generation systems, the nine regional reference and research library resource systems that were formed in the late 1960s to provide a structure for cooperation among academic libraries, special libraries, and the public library systems. These reference and research systems, which did not receive statutory authority until 1978, are still too underfunded to provide such full system support as union catalogs (although most are working on union lists of serials), consultant services, and a uniform level of interlibrary loan.

Why Share?

Resource-sharing systems spring from mixed parenthood. The ideal of equal opportunity of access is perhaps less a force in their birth than grudging acceptance that more information in more media is on the market than any library can afford to buy, process, and store. And although all libraries still rightly prefer to own what they need for the majority of their primary clientele, they are forced to find the rest elsewhere or not fill some of the needs and demands of their users. Resource sharing's time has come.

It is understandable, and perhaps right, that access to information is most readily available to the advanced researcher. Expression of serious purpose will open most doors to rare and restricted collections whether for direct access or interlibrary loan. Working within a long time frame makes it possible for even creaky loan mechanisms to produce results. Similarly, it is most practical for libraries to cooperate in the acquisition of bulky esoteric material that is likely to be little used.

But what does this have to do with young people? Exactly. Resource sharing is being built on a traditional model that may be ideal for researchers but may be only the first part of the full connection between local library services for youth.

Local Library Service to Youth

Most of the information needs young people bring to the library are for school-related materials on a relatively introductory level, and often the information is for an assignment due the next morning. Even if there is time, what librarian can lend curriculum-related material to one student when every school around is on the same schedule of topics?

The educational system's homework assignments themselves are frustrating to school librarians, who would prefer to expand curriculum horizons with multimedia and a personalized approach. But too often the teaching method appears to reduce the perceived need for librarians; too many schools are finding librarians expendable in the pressure to cut budgets.

The public libraries are, perhaps, equally uncertain as to how best to serve youth. Resistance to collecting curriculum-related materials breaks down when young users need material either nonexistent in their schools or locked up after three o'clock. Recognizing that young people's real information needs are much broader than finding the answers to home-work, some youth services librarians try to create an environment conducive to open discussion; others organize career and job information services. But in public libraries, too, budget cuts often result in reductions in specialized services to youth.

Young people are in danger of losing basic services at their library access points in schools and public libraries just as these libraries have increased opportunity to expand access to a greater pool of resources. If the basics are not provided at each access point—most-used materials, sufficient hours of service, and librarians to act as intermediaries between the inquirer and information sources—the concept of resource sharing is meaningless.

Interlibrary Loan

Interesting things are happening in the INTERSHARE pilots that give some indication of what might develop. Pilot law and regulations require building of automated union catalogs and delivery and other means of facilitating interlibrary loan. The "typical system" described earlier gives some idea of how inter-library loan has increased among school libraries from virtu-ally none to a volume varying from hundreds to thousands per school system in a few years. Analysis shows that an average of 80 percent of loans are filled within the school library system, but that balanced two-way loan is also growing between school libraries and public libraries and between school libraries and academic libraries. Considering that the interlibrary loan model for resource sharing comes from reference and research needs of adults, it is not surprising that quite a bit of borrowing is for faculty and administrators. This is not inappropriate, and the trickle-down theory provides hope that the educational ex-perience of young people will be better for it.

One barrier to interlibrary loan slowly being overcome is the usual one of lack of location tools. With the appearance of school library system holdings online, their materials suddenly become accessible to others using the same data base. The New York City School Library System, which is building its union catalog on the data base used by most of the public libraries in the city, because it considers them its first backup, became still more accessible to others following the publication of its three-volume book catalog.

The Yonkers School Library System, which is an OCLC Interlibrary Loan Subsystem participant, immediately began filling requests from around the country. Joint union catalog publication in microfiche form of the Westchester school library systems (Yonkers and the Putnam/Northern Westchester BOCES), opened their collections to non-OCLC libraries in the region.

Although the Westchester school library systems' COM CAT and the New York City School Library System's book catalog are location tools for librarians first, they have wonderful potential secondary uses. Because they are produced in the same format as the public libraries' catalogs in their area, young people who have learned how to use either the school or public libraries' catalog can make an easy and comfortable approach to the other.

In school library systems, portability of the book catalog or COM CAT makes it possible to bring knowledge of the library system's resources to curriculum committees or the teacher making lesson plans. The book catalog format, in particular, because it requires no equipment, is an extraordinary tool for outreach to teachers, who underutilize library resources in their teaching, and a highly visible aid in trying to convince administrators of the educational wealth of the library.

Beyond Interlibrary Loan

With limited funds almost totally dedicated to building data bases, communication, and start-up of interlibrary loan, there has been relatively little emphasis on formal linking of other kinds of services. On the other hand, the bringing together of public and school librarians who serve the same young people leads naturally to brainstorming of ways to do things together. It is possible that there is greater potential for improved library service to young people through coordination of other aspects of service than through the interlibrary loan service with which networking has begun.

Interlibrary loan is, of course, the moving of hard copy from place to place on demand. The costs involved are, in effect, the price of temporary acquisition of material the library has not bought, processed, and stored. Considering how impossibly large a collection would have to be in order to guarantee that anything that might ever be requested would be available, interlibrary loan at any price is likely to be a bargain.

Allowing the patron with the request direct access to requested material in another library is a sometimes preferable alternative to moving the material to the user. The same bibliographic tools and procedures as in interlibrary loan are used, but if the user has the mobility and time, going to the information is faster than borrowing. In some cases, young people might be served best with the assurance that material is at another accessible library. Unfortunately, for security reasons, schools tend not to encourage outsiders in. Therefore, user movement is likely to be one-way in the direction of the public library and whatever other libraries will welcome youth.

Access to school library materials is also usually limited, even for students, to school hours. To increase access to that material, several of the RARE pilots experimented with deposit of books that were on summer reading lists in nearby public libraries, thus adding several months a year to the service their books were providing. Jurisdictional problems are greater with deposits than with interlibrary loan, and questions such as who has responsibility for lost materials need to be solved in an equitable way.

Only when libraries can assume that material will be in the union catalog and readily available through loan or direct access can they be comfortable with coordinated collection development. But given that accessibility, it becomes possible for libraries of all types to specialize in a meaningful way. Public libraries should be able to devote their limited budgets to the variety of noncurricular and recreational materials that might enable young people to follow out-of-school individual interests of all kinds, while school libraries focus on the curricular needs of the majority of their students. Slow readers, or those new to English, could have access to materials from schools on a lower level. The gifted, or those who have read everything school and public libraries have to offer on their interest of the moment, could benefit from access to materials in academic and special libraries of all kinds.

Beyond Materials

Taking resource sharing beyond the materials-oriented interlibrary loan, direct access, and coordinated collection development opens the possibility of service to youth on a different level of information transfer. In developing the INTERSHARE network, even before interlibrary loan agreements and a delivery system were in place, two different telephone information programs were operational. The first was LIBRARY-ON-CALL, the extension of a traditional high-quality telephone reference service to the whole region after other telephone reference services closed down. The service is offered from 5 to 10 P.M. Monday through Thursday; 10 to 6 on Saturday; and 1 to 5 on Sunday.

Because librarians serving young people felt that telephone reference could short-circuit the educational process intended by teachers in assigning homework, another parallel telephone service was established. HOMEWORK-HOTLINE does not give quick answers to questions but, rather, helps young people or their parents understand the assignment and provides information on how to find answers. Offered 5–8 P.M. Monday through Thursday and staffed by school and public library personnel, HOMEWORK-HOTLINE offers a new service in a new medium to the youth who are the responsibility of both school and public libraries.

Each of these services is available from one site to the eight million people in the six counties of metropolitan New York. The location of the service is not germane to the immediacy of the service, since telecommunications can make any site a local call away. By centralizing the service, a small staff can serve far more potential callers in a cost-effective manner.

Using the same rationale, the INTERSHARE network produced and placed thousands of posters and car cards advertising library services in buses and subways all over the region. The 1982 campaign poster showed a ferocious purple lion looming over a child holding its leash and a book to illustrate:

Need to know what you are doing? Check in with your LI-BRARY . . . check out with the FACTS . . . Whether you need to select a doctor . . . tie a knot . . . learn long division . . . make a business decision . . . take a vacation . . . repair a car . . . or even tame a lion, your librarian can help you find the facts.

Making the library better known as a resource is the concern of all types of libraries. Therefore, activities fostering library awareness in a geographic area are natural cooperative activities of libraries within that area.

The Future

Concentrating on effective information transfer to the population served by the network should keep cooperating libraries alert to the potential of new technology in information transfer. Because young people are more open than any other segment of the population to new technology, librarians who seek to serve them have reason to try to remain equally open to new possibilities of service.

The school library system and network pilot projects in New York State are at a crucial juncture in their lives. Authorization and funding expired on June 30, 1983. Those of us who have worked in them are convinced that they have just begun to show what they can do and the difference they will make in service to everyone. Library services that young people have come to rely on are the ones they will use and vote for in the years ahead.

Notes

1. *Toward a National Program for Library and Information Services: Goals for Action* (Washington, D.C.: U.S. National Commission on Libraries and Information Science, 1975), p. xi.
2. *Library Service to the People of New York State* (Albany, N.Y.: University of the State of New York, State Education Department, 1982), p. 11.
3. *NYSILL Manual* (Albany, N.Y.: University of the State of New York, State Education Department, New York State Interlibrary Loan Network, 1970), p. 5.
4. Ibid., p. 7.
5. *Effective Connections* (Albany, N.Y.: University of the State of New York, State Education Department, 1983), pp. 7–8.

14
College/Library Cooperation: The Queensboro Hill Project

BRUCE A. SHUMAN

For almost a decade the building just sat there. Construction had been completed in the early 1970s, but the funds were lacking to finish the wiring and the plumbing and to staff and operate the branch. Residents of the community grew restless, then discontented, besieging the system's headquarters with requests and demands for fulfillment of the promise to the neighborhood that the building represented. Then the money was in place and plans were made to open the new branch.

The opportunity for innovation presented itself. System planners wanted the branch to be formatted along the lines of a modern bookstore, with display shelving, making it possible for many materials to be shown face-out. An attractive, colorful, clean, well-lighted place was designed to do two things: to take care of the normal requirements of a heterogeneous urban community's residents and, as a special point of emphasis, to serve as a magnet and resource for the young adult population.

Just across the expressway from the branch location is one of the eighteen campuses of the sprawling City University of New York. One of the signal points of the college's mission

was involvement in the community, and the impending opening of a new branch in its backyard seemed a fortuitous opportunity to make good on that mission. When it was learned
that the branch was to open in mid-1982 as an innovative,
demonstration library facility, the president of the college,
together with members of the faculty of the library school,
sought to get involved.

This report is a description and analysis of the planning, the
execution, and the results (to date) of a joint effort between the
Queens Borough Public Library and Queens College Graduate
School of Library and Information Studies: the Queensboro
Hill Project.

The project came about through common interest. The
Queens Borough Public Library wanted a young adult center in
the northern sector of the borough in order to complement the
main library's teenage services, located in the southern part of
Queens. Further, as already mentioned, the library sought a
vehicle for several new merchandising techniques that it was
eager to try out without the cost and labor of renovating an existing structure: a demonstration center for young adult services. The location of the branch, a few short blocks from a
major high school and junior high school, is ideal as a young
adult magnet, and transportation to and from the branch to
most parts of Queens is convenient.

Queens College sought involvement in its community and a
chance to contribute to the educational opportunity of citizens
of Queens (and beyond) who were not actually enrolled in
courses. The Graduate School of Library and Information
Studies wanted a training center for students, through internships and/or paid employment in a nearby public library facility, a chance for students to put academic training to use in an
actual library situation.

Both sides welcomed the opportunity for joint planning,
which would serve to build bridges between the library and the
college and to form relationships between and among their personnel. All that remained was to decide what was to be done
through such coordinated planning and to identify sources of
funding for "enhanced and enriched services." The branch was
to open in any event, but the involvement of Queens College,
and the funds such involvement produced, made it possible for
the provision of greatly augmented young adult services to the
concentric communities of Queensboro Hill, Flushing,
Queens, and, ultimately, the New York City metropolitan area.

In fall 1981, therefore, a planning committee, composed of members of the Queens Borough Public Library staff and Queens College library school faculty, began holding periodic meetings for the purposes of constructing a budget, aimed at provision of those enhanced and augmented services for young adults, and for coordinating the disbursement of the funds when they were received.

The original budget was grandiose in concept, calling for $90,000 to be spent in the first year of the project, with a matching amount to follow for the second year. It was divided among personnel costs and materials and featured several automated services designed to assist young people in selecting colleges, choosing occupations, getting financial aid, and finding out about alternative paths of professional advancement. The budget was submitted to the state legislature in Albany, where it went through the almost inevitable process of arbitration and compromise, over a period of several months. After this time of anxious waiting and worrying, the planning team was gratified (all things considered) to receive the go-ahead to begin spending the sum of $35,000 for Year I of the project. Although much had been taken from the initial scheme of turning Queensboro Hill into a superbranch, with all manner of high-powered and valuable services and collections, much remained, and hasty plans were drawn up to disburse the $35,000 before time ran out on the fiscal year.

The Disbursement of Year-I Funds

The Guidance Information System

The Guidance Information System (GIS) is an interactive, online service offered by the TSC Company, a subsidiary of Houghton Mifflin. GIS permits the student, through the use of a trained search intermediary, to access up-to-date information about four postsecondary educational choices—four-year colleges, two-year colleges, graduate schools, and occupations—with current information on every field listed in the *Dictionary of Occupational Titles* and the *Occupational Outlook Handbook*. The service permits the user to tailor the search, homing in on the desired information through the gradual, stepwise narrowing of search terms.

Although GIS is a very efficient means for a student to ob-

Queensboro Hill Project Budget (finalized) for Year I:
1982/1983 (figures approximate)

Guidance Information System	$5,000
166 hours of online computer time for Guidance Information System	5,000
Telephone installation and first month's bill	160
Computer paper	113
Young Adult career materials	3,168
Young Adult paperback collection*	2,800
Ethnic materials (and selection consultant's honorarium)	2,500
Processing of materials by Queens Borough Public Library	455
Insurance on hardware	250
Videocassette collection	5,000
Videocassette player and stand, with locking case	1,732
Subscriptions to *Magazine Index* and *National Newspaper Index*, with microreaders for both	3,750
Community survey (personnel costs)	5,000
	$35,000

*In English and Spanish.

Note: No amount may exceed $5,000 by state law under the regulations of the City University of New York. Amounts higher require a special resolution of the Board of Regents, and the planning team thought it best to scale down all sums to fall within the CUNY guidelines.

tain information, it is not inexpensive; time on GIS sells for $30 per hour, with telecommunications charges costing extra. During its first year, the service is being used infrequently, but advertising is scheduled boroughwide, and use is expected to pick up shortly. Included in the basic cost of the system are a video terminal and a printer, which can serve as a print terminal itself. In Year II the Queens Borough Public Library system stands ready to augment or diminish the 166 hours of online time deemed adequate for the initial year, based on prior usage statistics.

Young adult career materials

Extra funds made it possible for the branch to acquire and make available multiple copies of popular and timely books and other materials dealing with getting a job, so that many people can borrow the same materials at the same time. Topics such as successful letters, interviews, resumes, and interpersonal relations are covered in depth. There are also individual titles on numerous career fields, with strong coverage in preparation for higher education and specialized professions.

Young adult paperback collection

The young adult paperback collection was envisioned as providing recreational and cultural enrichment reading for teenagers, in both English and Spanish. Emphasis is on high-interest, easy-vocabulary materials, but numerous classics were purchased, as well. The books are arranged on display shelves in bookstore fashion, face-out, to attract readers by means of colorful, illustrated covers and to encourage and facilitate browsing. Multiple copies of popular titles were purchased, but no attempt was made to preserve the books with permabindings. Expendable but eye-catching, this collection has proven to be immensely popular with young people who just happen to drop into the library on their way home or while waiting for a bus.

An ad hoc Queensboro Hill reading project was devised to encourage young people to read numbers of these enrichment materials. Awards took the form of boxes of Munchkins, small round doughnuts provided by a local Dunkin Donuts store. Future plans include several meet-the-author programs and certificates of achievement for reading lists of books provided by the Queens Borough Public Library.

Ethnic materials

Queens is, arguably, the most ethnically diverse of New York's five boroughs. The population of the borough is varied, and virtually all of the United Nations are represented. It therefore seemed appropriate that a fraction of the money for the project be spent in acquiring a good, general collection of multiethnic reference materials and at least some representation of each of the ethnic groups residing in Queens. In this connection, the project was fortunate in having available the services of a consultant who had spent many years selecting and using ethnic materials and whose contributions ensured adequate representation in the collection.

Processing of materials

It was determined that the project funding should contain a specified amount to compensate the Queens Borough Public Library for the cost of entering the new materials, technically the property of Queens College, into the computerized listing of holdings for the system. This charge was assessed at the rate of $1.30 per title, or $455 for all the new materials acquired through the project.

Insurance on hardware

Since videocassettes and ancillary playback equipment are on the list of easily fenced items, and given that several plate glass windows in the building could not be said to constitute airtight security, the college's legal advisers determined that the branch might fall victim to vandals and thieves. The college, therefore, decided to purchase (at $250 per year) all-risk coverage for the project's computer and videocassette equipment. Such coverage would not only protect the college's investment but would also allay anxiety on the part of the library system that its liability might extend to the college's purchases.

Feature films

One service that was added to the project, to the unanimous acclaim of neighborhood residents, was a collection of feature films, available on convenient videocassettes, in the VHS format. Eighty-five of these films were purchased in the first year, with approximately 130 more slated for Year II.

Reference materials

Magazine Index and *National Newspaper Index* are two extremely valuable publications that, in the best of all possible worlds, should be available in every branch of a system such as Queens Borough. *Magazine Index* has several advantages over the more familiar and more ubiquitous *Reader's Guide*. It indexes over twice as many periodicals on a regular basis, and it cumulates: Each issue contains complete indexing since 1976, resulting in only one place to look for an entry. Unfortunately, not only are these services expensive but they are available only in microfilm and online editions, necessitating the purchase or rental of hardware for their use. *National Newspaper Index*, which indexes five major newspapers, is similarly expensive and available only in nonconventional formats. But the cooperation, and funds, of Queens College have made it possible for the small and modest Queensboro Hill branch to have such big-league services as these available for reference service; in subsequent years, budgeting for these materials is to be picked up by the Queens Borough Public Library.

Community survey

One important addition to the list of services that both sides found to be important was a community survey, in two parts, to test the impact of the new branch on its neighborhood residents. Part I, undertaken immediately prior to the opening of the facility, was to explore the wants and expectations of community residents, as well as serving as a form of advertising for the grand opening of the new branch on June 14, 1982.

The present author was designated as principal investigator in the survey. The budget provided for five part-time assistants to participate in both the canvassing of the community's residents and the compilation and interpretation of data over a three-week period. The project was carried out in the Graduate School of Library and Information Studies, approximately one-half mile from the branch. Approximately 10 percent of the interviews were personally conducted by survey team members on the streets, but most people were interviewed by telephone in their homes. Some 496 respondents were asked a brief set of questions designed to elicit their feelings regarding the new branch.

The survey revealed that 188 homes had children in them, with an average of approximately two children per home. Because the area covered by the Queensboro Hill branch is small, everyone lived reasonably close to the branch, and a wide spectrum of the community had been alerted to what was soon to be available to their children. The survey also made the library aware that in its eagerness to attract the young, it had, to a large extent, neglected the sizable population of older persons in its vicinity—15 percent of the respondents to the survey. (Such an oversight is correctable, and will be attended to in future years of the branch's operation.)

Another survey finding, which was not so surprising, was that a large proportion of the area's people read in foreign languages, and that among these, Italian, Spanish, German, and Chinese were most commonly indicated. The implication of this findng was clear enough, and more titles in these languages were ordered in the second year of operation. Of course, Queensboro Hill is only one of almost five dozen branches in the system. Among the branches that specialize in foreign-

Queensboro Hill Project Proposed Budget for Year II
(January 1983) (figures approximate)

Continuation, updated career materials collection	$ 7,000
Continuation, expansion of videocassette collection	9,000
Continuation, GIS system (100 hours @ $35)	3,500
Service contract for GIS	500
Computer literacy workshops (2 instructors)	4,000
Microcomputers with printers (5)	10,000
Software (assorted programs)	3,000
Service contract for microcomputers	1,000
Updated and expanded computer book collection	5,000
English-as-a-second-language classes (2 instructors)	2,000
User/community survey	2,000
Publicity, advertising, postage	2,000
Staff development programs for Queens Borough Public Library employees	4,000
Tuition to Queens College for those enrolled in staff development programs	4,500
Cooperative education program, providing for paid intern(s) to work in branch from Graduate School of Library and Information Studies, salary and benefits for 6 months	7,500
Joint programming at branch (honoraria and custodial services)	5,000
Student or clerical staff to assist with new services	5,000
	$75,000*

*Amount and services subject to modification by New York State Legislature.

language collections is the Central Library of the system, some four to five miles away.

The Budget for Year II

As previously noted, the emphasis of the first year's planning and disbursement was young adult services, and such a focus has carried over into the budget for Year II. Future money secured for the project, if available, will be earmarked for remedying the gaps and omissions of the initial budget. Ideally, all services purchased with the teenage audience in mind have much wider application and appeal than strictly to the twelve to twenty age group. Year II's budget contains money for Part II of the survey, which will attempt to determine the impact of the branch approximately one year after it opened. Residents and users will be asked about the use they actually make of the branch and its services and facilities, rather than what they plan or hope to do with them. Results should be illuminating as the focus shifts from user survey to use survey; the summer of 1983 is targeted for the conduct of this follow-up study.

At present, the budget for the second year of operation is undergoing the tortuous route through the New York State Legislature, which will not be done with it for several months. According to the preliminary budget some services are to continue, some are to become the responsibility of the public library system, and several new ideas are to be tried.

Year I in Review

In summing up the first year of the Queensboro Hill cooperative project, the author would like to present a few of the salient aspects of the joint experience for the benefit of those contemplating similar ventures:

1. When a college interacts with a community resource, such as a public library system, dealings between academic and library planners offer the opportunity for each side to understand the problems of the other and to share in an activity that is beneficial to all concerned. Once a successful precedent has been established, future occasions for joint planning are more readily envisioned.

2. The old adage about "Too many cooks" is quite true, when more than three persons from each side get together to establish criteria, work out a budget, and decide who is to do what, and when. Each side should appoint one person whose job is (temporarily) modified to include primary responsibility for the project, and all scheduling and decision making should involve those two designated individuals, who, it is hoped, work well and synergistically together. Other interested parties should be involved as the situation requires, but the day-to-day management of the project ought to be in a few competent hands.

3. In any new venture, experimentation will take place. At such times, it is important to observe closely the reaction of the intended audience to the services provided. Then, after a decent interval, tinkering with the initial mix of services, or emphasis placed on each, may begin. Perhaps most important of all, from the initial moment of planning to the gala opening day (and well beyond) is the need for a mechanism whereby the

planning team gathers and analyzes community input. Keep asking people what they want, what could be done to make it better, what they get that they don't want or need, and what's missing. Stand ready to modify the project periodically (or as needed) to incorporate feedback into subsequent planning and disbursement of funds. Don't be afraid to scrap or redesign the entire project, but be certain that there are serious problems before you consider drastic remedies. Communication is the most important criterion of effective joint programs; without it, they cannot succeed, but with it, most things are possible.

4. Try to keep budgetary matters as simple and as consistent with requirements as possible. Complications result when one institution does accounting procedures for goods and commodities that are delivered to another, as was the case with the Queensboro Hill Project. Still, people of goodwill and infinite patience and cheer can overcome administrative hurdles and problems with delay, regulations, signatures (and countersignatures), and authority.

Remember, too, that if joint projects work, and work effectively, there will be favorable publicity and the strong promise of future emoluments for both participating agencies. If the project fails, blame will normally be placed at various doorsteps, but at fault, most likely, will be poor planning and poor coordination.

Those responsible for this project, aimed at providing many and various services to the young people of a vast urban area of the largest city in the United States, are proud of what has happened thus far and hopeful about the future.

IV
Professional Development

15
Library Education for Young Adult Specialists

JOAN L. ATKINSON

Pre-service education is what most students expect of library schools and what most library schools direct their resources toward. The flexibility of library schools to choose how they will use their resources is, however, more restricted than students and practitioners sometimes realize. This chapter will begin, then, with a discussion of the political environment of library education. Once that is established, a total program for the education of the young adult specialist will be presented along with a practical look at what can be accomplished in a young adult materials and services course.

The Struggle for Survival

To say that library schools feel threatened in the early 1980s is an understatement. Although several schools are rumored to be barely hanging on, the first American Library Association– accredited program to announce a closing date in this decade was that of the State University of New York College at Geneseo, accredited since 1946; that closing date was August 1983. Geneseo's president regretted the "programmatic decision," which apparently came as a result of declining enrollments.[1]

Other ALA-accredited programs to face threats of elimination are those at the University of Minnesota, which ceased admitting new students in June 1982 but may resume operations if the university approves a restructured program, and the University of Missouri at Columbia, whose proposed elimination elicited hundreds of support letters to legislators from students, alumni, library associations, and friends.[2] Program restructuring has already taken place at Rutgers, where the library school and the school of communications merged in fall 1982. A similar merger, but in this instance with computing science, appears to be underway at the University of Mississippi. Even Columbia University's prestigious and richly endowed library education program is the subject of scrutiny by a committee charged to make recommendations about the future mission of the school.

Declining enrollment is probably the single most important factor accounting for the survival struggles of ALA-accredited MLS programs. The decline in enrolled students is, however, only one part of the picture. It is matched by another demographic reality: the decline in the number of placements of graduates in library positions. Of 1981 graduates of accredited programs, 2,863 were placed in library positions.[3] According to the *Bowker Annual*, this figure is down from 2,898 in 1980, 3,371 in 1979, and 3,393 in 1978. The peak year for placements was 1974, with 3,891. In fact, the 1981 placement figure was the lowest since 1966, when there were approximately the same number, 2,865.[4]

The increased competition for students between 1966 and 1981 is, however, another very important factor in the current survival struggle. In 1966 there were thirty-five schools reporting placements; in 1981 there were sixty-five schools reporting. In other words, almost twice the number of schools were placing the same number of graduates. With a diminished pool of students and a proliferation of programs, the handwriting on the wall is obvious. All presently accredited programs cannot survive without a redefinition of mission and reallocation of resources.

How the reallocation of resources has affected or will affect the young adult specialty is not absolutely clear. One thing that is clear, however, is that students entering library education programs are very pragmatic. They want jobs when they get out, and their perception is that the job market demands training in the use of electronic technology. Few students, except those taking a tightly prescribed school certification program, go through education programs now without taking data-base searching, library automation, and other courses that include a strong component in computer applications to library functions. In the face of this demand, the library schools' resources are being deployed to add computers, terminals, printers, information processing laboratories and the necessary software to use it all. Faculty resources also are being shifted toward operating and teaching the new systems.

For the young adult specialization, these changes have some positive outcomes. New professionals are likely to feel comfortable with microcomputers, software, programming languages, and electronic communications systems at a time when library-using young adults are likely to want and need guidance in the use of these informational and recreational sources. As faculty positions are reallocated, however, the young adult specialty overall is likely to suffer. Full-time positions and tenure-earning positions for those whose priority is the specialty are apt to be nil.

Some young adult practitioners may actually perceive a profit in this arrangement. After all, there is a great deal to be said for the use of practicing young adult specialists as adjunct faculty. They bring a practical, working knowledge of the service that is difficult for full-time faculty to maintain, since they are several years separated from direct service and are encouraged by their institutions and by ALA accreditation standards to spend their time doing research and emphasizing academic achievement.

Although something may be gained in terms of the young adult materials and services course, a great deal is apt to be lost to the specialty in general. The specialty is subject to invisibility in library schools, where there is no regular faculty member in faculty meetings speaking on its behalf or representing the interest of the specialty in curriculum committee meetings and in collection development meetings. Nor is there a regular faculty member on committees planning colloquia, inviting guest lecturers to campus, voting on awards, deciding on the validity of internships, and making dozens of small decisions day after day. Furthermore, research that the field needs to establish its importance and evaluate its performance is more likely to come from full-time, permanent library school faculty than from any other one source. They are in the best position to write grant proposals, to get release time to carry out research projects, and to be rewarded for the dissemination of research.

Librarians have always operated in a potentially volatile political environment, a fact they cannot afford to forget. In addition, within libraries some functions and services are traditionally better established than others. The young adult specialty is and has always been a threatened or ignored service in most parts of the country. Talk of curtailing or eliminating services, then, is nothing new to young adult librarians. Even so, young adult specialists are not apt to empathize with threatened library education programs and the professors associated with them any more than library educators are apt to empathize with threatened young adult service programs and the practitioners associated with them. Each group is likely to think of the other as more in control of decision making than it is. The result is a certain level of frustration and a tendency to blame the other for a situation that is genuinely catch-22. Library schools cannot ensure the survival of the young adult specialty in public libraries any more than practicing young adult librarians can ensure the survival of the specialty in library schools. Adaptation to the political environment is absolutely crucial to both because each is an endangered species.

The Political Environment

Political theorists and system analysts are interested in knowing why some organizations flourish while others die away. Librarians in general and especially those in endangered services have a lot to gain from literature on political systems theory and organizational behavior. David Easton, a political scientist, suggests that the persistence of a political system depends upon its capacity to receive and respond to feedback from its environment at the same time it influences that environment by its outputs into it.[5] This kind of system is called an open system because it recognizes the necessity of a continuous flow of information and effects between system and environment. The contrast to this organizational structure is a closed system or a pure rationality model in which the system sets its own goals and deploys its resources directly toward the achievement of those goals without taking into account pressures from the environment.[6]

Young adult specialists and library educators dream of living just one day in a closed system. In such a system, a young adult librarian who set the goal of getting accurate and appropriate career information to every young adult aged fourteen to seventeen would find all the needed information available at all readability levels and in all formats at affordable prices; staff would be able and willing to interact positively with all young adults; the director would assign no other tasks that would conflict with planning school visits or programs to get the word out. In a closed system, a library educator who set the goal of performing research to document the necessity of the young adult specialty would find all data available and money forthcoming to pay for gathering it; all other faculty would understand the importance of the project and be supportive; the dean would assign no teaching or committee responsibilities to conflict with report writing and dissemination of the findings.

Reality is, however, that both groups work in open systems, which constantly deflect a great deal of organizational energy away from achieving established goals and toward putting out a hundred and one brushfires. For library education the external and internal pressures that threaten the organization are legion.

The library school is one unit in the university structure, scrambling for university funds, for enrollments, for its share of scholarships and work-study students, for research grants, for recognition gained through visibility on university committees, for admission standards that potentially bring it into conflict with other units of the university, for tenure and promotion for its faculty, for understanding that the service function is particularly important in a professional school, and on and on.

Within publicly supported education and within the state library structure, the library school is also scrambling—for preeminence among all the schools in the state that offer library education programs, for state certification of its program, for support by the state library organizations, for employers to hire its graduates, for a voice in the designing of state competency examinations for graduates, for a voice in decisions about networking, for ways to cooperate with the state library agency and on and on. Beyond the state library structure is the state's political structure, the need to work within the bounds of current legislative constraints but also to influence future legislation.

The national scene, too, constrains the school's actions. National library organizations set standards, accredit or disaccredit programs, define the mission of libraries, and offer opportunities for service to the profession and for continuing education. The national political and economic scene influences the availability of jobs, of research grants, and of federal funding for state and local projects.

Finally, for every library school there are individuals who constrain the power over decision making—such as alumni, friends, benefactors, employers of graduates, and former faculty. Since the library school functions as an open system, it must continually take into account the demands from its environment and balance conflicting demands so that no environmental entity is totally alienated. To do otherwise is to place survival in jeopardy.

Maintaining a balance among conflicting demands, however, is not easy. What is the school to do, for example, when an influential person in the state library community recommends a prospective student who scores only 800 points on the Graduate Record Examination? Institutional standards suggest 1,000 points, but the university is also concerned about enrollments so its interest in the decision is ambiguous. ALA accreditation might ultimately be affected if very many students with below-standard scores were admitted, but one score is not likely to have a decisive effect. Another consideration is how the field will be ultimately affected. If the low-scoring applicant gets through the school's program and is a disaster as a practitioner, the school gets the reputation of producing incompetents. This is only one of any number of possible examples of a library school's attempt to respond to conflicting messages from its environment.

Besides these external factors, there are internal considerations. Continuing the above example, will qualified students suffer while instructional time is diverted to pull the low achiever along? Will the low-scoring student be a drag in class, one who slows the pace of the class by asking superfluous and time-consuming questions and by complaining about the burden of work?

As suggested in the above example, there are almost as many internal as external constraints on a library school's control over its decisions and performance. The number of faculty members and their abilities, motivations, rank, and tenure influence what the school can hope to achieve. The administration of the school is constrained by its budget, the number of staff members employed, their organizational assignments, school policies, and the committee and advising structure. Students, too, influence decisions by their number, abilities, and demands. Adequate facilities for classrooms, laboratories, information processing, and colloquia influence the school's program, as does availability of instructional and library materials. Finally the curriculum, particularly the number of required courses and their sequencing, constrains other decisions, such as scheduling of electives and admitting students more than once or twice a calendar year.

If a library school has made the internal decision to employ a professor who cares about the young adult specialization, that person is forced to make painful choices about allocation of professional time. Virtually no educator gets to teach in just one specialization. The young adult educator may also be teaching children's materials, selection, public libraries, reference, instructional design, school media services, or any of a host of possibilities. Preparation time must be divided accordingly.

The university reward structure must also be taken into account. Traditionally, universities have evaluated professional school faculties in three areas: teaching, research, and service. Though the relative weight assigned each area changed from institution to institution, a faculty member was generally expected to make some contribution to all three and to excel in at least two of the areas. In recent years, however, there has been a decided change—a shift away from emphasis on public service and toward emphasis on research, with teaching remaining a given.[7]

For more educators in the young adult specialization, the emphasis on teaching presents no philosophical conflict. They place a high priority on the teaching function and attempt to keep up with new literature and materials, as well as current practice. Keeping abreast of new developments is no mean achievement in a field where materials change dramatically over a short period of time. Sometimes, however, in the university setting good teaching is taken for granted. Working hard at it seems to get the professor little recognition; it is only when it is done poorly that it tends to be noticed and then, of course, it is a mark against the educator.

The university's emphasis on research is another matter.

Both annual evaluations and reviews conducted at crucial junctures when tenure and promotion decisions are made tend to emphasize the research function of the university, and it is the area of research that appears to cause young adult educators most grief. If they choose practical topics, with the goal of speaking to current practice, the university is likely to see the result as lacking the theoretical orientation that it values. If they choose highly theoretical topics, who wants to read their results and where are they to be published? In the young adult field the journals most valued by practitioners, *Voice of Youth Advocates*, *Top of the News*, and *School Library Journal*, simply do not focus on research and certainly not on statistical analyses, accompanied by charts and graphs and written in the scholarly style that the university is likely to assess as excellent.

A perfect example is Shirley Fitzgibbons' excellent summary of applied research for the young adult area, which should be read by every young adult practitioner, public library administrator, and young adult educator. This extremely important article is published in *Emergency Librarian*, a Canadian journal with a circulation of 3,000.[8] Valuable as the journal is, it simply cannot give the information the breadth of dissemination it deserves, and yet one wonders what journal has the scope and readership to have done better. Overall, the university expects professors to do the kind of research and get published in the kinds of journals that young adult practitioners don't want to read.

Another complication for the young adult educator is that, especially in an economic climate of cutbacks and scarce resources, universities bolster their budgets by encouraging externally funded research, which brings in outside dollars. The university's agenda of getting grant money, carrying out research projects, and disseminating results is likely to be at odds with the field's agenda for the young adult educator, which is to benefit current practice in a tangible way.

In other words, the field's agenda places an emphasis on the public service function that is out of synchronization with the university's perceived mission. Being active in public service means for the young adult educator accepting leadership in such diverse activities as planning continuing education programs, participating in state and national association decision making, reviewing and recommending new materials, helping to head off censorship activity, editing how-to-do-it-good newsletters, and coordinating internships. Sometimes services like these are rewarded in the university structure; sometimes they are not. In a way, the conscientious young adult educator cannot win: Forced choices alienate one constituency or the other. Common sense ultimately dictates that the constituency that issues the paychecks gets to decide how time will be allocated.

This picture of the political environment of library education is presented to lower expectations about what library schools can do for the young adult specialty. It does not hurt to have expectations lowered if the higher cannot be attained. In fact it helps to eliminate frustration. Analogous to *One Flew Over the Cuckoo's Nest*, this picture of library education tries to demonstrate the presence of "Big Nurse" in our lives.

A Program for the Young Adult Specialist

Few students enter library schools with the intention of training themselves to be young adult specialists. Political environments are of as much consequence to them as to educators. They generally want to know where the jobs are and how to cover all the bases to be minimally credentialed for whatever becomes available in their preferred geographic area at the moment they graduate. But whether or not there is a vocal contingency clamoring for young adult training, library schools need a plan for offering that training.

Professional literature has been dealing with this topic for more than fifty years, with astonishingly similar criticisms and suggestions. Susan Steinfirst skillfully presents and documents the historical record in her 1979 article, "Education of the Young Adult Librarian."[9] As early as 1930, Jean Roos of the Cleveland Public Library enumerated four expectations a library might have of a person specially trained to work with adolescents. They include commitment, understanding of young people, knowledge of the reading process, and administrative ability. She described a program for meeting these expectations and called for standards more strenuous for the training of public librarians than for school librarians.[10]

Though such a set of standards has not been forthcoming during the intervening years, progress toward codifying a list of expectations continues. ALA's Young Adult Services Division in July 1982 approved a document called *Competencies for Li-*

brarians Serving Youth (reprinted in Appendix II of this volume).[11] Formulated by YASD's Education Committee, the document identifies seven general areas of training and lists behavioral objectives for each. The general areas—leadership and professionalism, knowledge of client group, communication, administration, knowledge of materials, access to information, and services—are those in which any pre-service librarian, regardless of specialization, would want a library school to offer training.

A strength of the competency list is that it looks at the output rather than the input dimension. It does not prescribe courses to be offered or recommend packaging the achievement of competencies in any set format. It simply says that a YA librarian needs skills and knowledge in several identifiable areas. Library schools are a proper place to begin getting them, although any realistic look at the list indicates the necessity of an ongoing plan for training beyond the fifth-year master's program.

The competency list is a valuable tool for library educators who are involved in curriculum planning and advising for the young adult specialty. Beside each behavioral objective, they may list courses currently offered in which that objective is likely to be met. It is important to involve faculty who are not particularly knowledgeable about the young adult specialty in this process. The competency list needs to be circulated to them with a request that they list their course number beside any competency which they feel that course helps to develop. After the results are gathered and tabulated, a list of courses that purport to enhance the development of these competencies will emerge. Also gaps will become apparent.

Discussion will follow on whether new library school courses need to be developed, whether courses offered by other departments in the university should be recommended, or whether the library educator's role is to encourage organizations that provide continuing education to offer training in those areas. Possibly some combination might also be developed: A state library group sponsors a program or workshop, which the library school cosponsors or endorses, or the library school cross-lists a course from another university division.

The YASD Education Committee is continuing its work to make the competency list more generally useful. Its plans are to develop model teaching activities at both pre-service and continuing education levels over the next two years and to find ways of disseminating these to both educators and practitioners.

According to national placement statistics on 1981 library school graduates, the young adult specialization was one of four areas in which demand for qualified applicants exceeded supply.[12] Unless low salaries is a major contributor to young adult positions remaining unfilled, this advantageous market may influence entering students to take seriously the possibility of training themselves for the specialty.

Meanwhile, if library schools fail to plan meaningful programs for students who know they want to be youth workers, they will do in the future what their counterparts did in the past: manipulate the regular curriculum to their advantage. The flexibility offered within many courses to select topics of personal interest for papers, research critiques, projects, bibliographies, and other assignments enables individuals committed to youth to take some control of their own training. It demands a bit more creativity and goal setting on their part to structure the links for themselves, but again the competency list provides a framework.

Steinfirst summarized the desired training program succinctly:

For over 45 years, the library profession has been requesting basically the same things in the training of YA librarians. They can be categorized as follows: some knowledge of the adolescent as a person (psychology) in a changing world (sociology); book knowledge (selection techniques and tools); knowledge of reading interests (methodology and theory); understanding of administration (management skills); practical experience (a practicum); and programming skills—all with emendations and additions dependent upon when the suggestions were made.[13]

The young adult course

At the heart of the young adult specialist's training program is the materials and services course, or courses, in a few library schools. This course needs to do at least three things: produce understanding of adolescent development and needs in relation to the current political and social climates; introduce literature, multimedia materials, and professional publications

174 PROFESSIONAL DEVELOPMENT

particular to the young adult specialty; and alert the student to current issues in both the materials and services areas.

It is indicative of the difficulty of achieving these results that no adequate textbook has been written for this course. A perusal of the course outlines of twenty-five educators who teach the course across the United States and Canada shows that most of them piece together readings from a variety of sources.[14]

For literature they may use Carlsen's *Books and the Teenage Reader*, Donelson and Nilsen's *Literature for Today's Young Adults*, Fader's *New Hooked on Books*, or New York Public Library's *Books for the Teen Age*. Probably Lenz and Mahood's *Young Adult Literature: Background and Criticism* does the best job of providing readings to meet the three needs, but it is not mentioned in the course outlines as a textbook. For selection, ALA's *Selecting Materials for Children and Young Adults* is frequently mentioned.

For services there is even less consensus. Some use Braverman's *Youth, Society and the Public Library*; others stick with Edwards' 1974 work, *The Fair Garden and the Swarm of Beasts*; some use YASD's overview of the service, *Directions for Library Service to Young Adults*. Some readings concentrate on particular services like Bodart's *Booktalk!* and LiBretto's *High/Low Handbook*. Occasionally readings related to research in the field, like YASD's *Media and the Young Adult*, are recommended. In the area of adolescent development, such a variety of readings are used that it is impossible to identify a corpus of agreed-upon works.

The absence of a textbook may seem to indicate an overall lack of development of a philosophical framework for the young adult course. This is not the case, however. Kingsbury's survey of practitioners and educators on their priorities as demonstrated by their assignment of hours of training desirable for a particular activity or concept shows essential agreement about the areas to be covered.[15]

A better explanation is that the materials, services, and issues related to the period of adolescence continue to be more ephemeral, elusive, and trendy than those related to children or adults. A textbook that attempts to freeze a state of the art at any one moment will smack of datedness almost immediately. The collage of readings actually serves to make a point about the specialty in general: It will be ever-changing, not subject to codification in a magnum opus.

For the educator, this means learning to live comfortably in a state of flux where course content is always evolving. It means that reading professional literature and attending national conferences are even more directly related to teaching than these activities may be for specialists in other areas. It means expecting to update the syllabus every time the course is offered and being flexible about adapting assignments if they do not seem to be meeting students' current needs. It means the course must never become stale or set, and in fact that it will always be a bit unmanageable.

As in the rest of library education, the educator must bridge the gap between the ideal and the actual. An example is the viewing of multimedia materials. Certainly it is desirable that students view current films and filmstrips, areas in which the production of quality materials is burgeoning. Library schools generally have low budgets, which prohibit purchase of more than a few of these expensive materials. Usually university libraries leave such purchases to film centers. In any case, the materials are not readily accessible. Rental is the educator's best alternative, a headache all around because first previewing is necessary, then finding a rental date convenient to both distributor and educator, then using and returning the materials promptly. Students who are absent or need more than one showing are just out of luck. The result may be a choice to view standard or representative films and filmstrips rather than the latest innovations or examples.

Even keeping a current book collection presents a problem for university libraries. Young adult titles are not generally represented in approval plans that the university library subscribes to. Individual orders seem to take forever to fill, and young adult books are understandably not top priority items in the university collection. The library school may try to supply current paperbacks, probably the most feasible alternative; however, important titles sometimes fail to come out in paperback. When they do there is usually a time lag between hardcover edition and paperback so that the library school class is without the most current, sometimes the most controversial, materials at the most teachable moment.

Although there is no teaching method for the young adult course that is necessarily superior to all others, an open system model of organizational behavior should be operative. Classes tend to be distinctive and different. Some have a level of maturity that elicits the professor's confidence that students can direct the class to suit their own needs. Other classes demand constant guidance and supervision and teacher talk to keep them focused on meaningful goals. Some classes are made up of neophytes for whom every idea is new; others are dominated by practitioners returning to update their credentials or to seek more advanced degrees. Some classes are full of people enthusiastic about the young adult specialty; others are composed of those who need to take a course, any course, at that day and hour. All of these variables influence the choice by the professor of a mode of class interaction and participation that will work best in that circumstance.

Overall it seems best for the young adult course to model the kind of balance between guidance and participation in decision making that foreshadows what students as effective practitioners will later use with young adults. In reading assignments, for instance, there should be flexibility for a student to pursue personal interests, but there should be a demand that certain types of literature and certain topics be explored as well. Although skills such as annotating, reviewing, compiling mediagraphies, and talking effectively are needed by all, they can be demonstrated quite differently, and the course to the extent possible depending on class size should allow for negotiating demands to meet perceived individual needs.

The topic of class size deserves a bit more elaboration. The shrinking enrollments per library school mean that except for core courses the size of classes is greatly reduced unless the course attracts students from other university departments. For the young adult course, though English and education students are potential enrollees, class size is likely to be small. Up to a point, to be small is a bonus; it allows for individualized instruction and intensity of student participation. On the other side, though, it reduces the number of diverse viewpoints that may be expressed, and, more important to the political process, reduces the possibility of a school's offering the course every semester or offering advanced electives in the specialty. After all, can a university afford to offer a course for only three, four, or five students?

Above all, whatever its size, the class should model openness to a diversity of viewpoints and respect for individuals holding different views. The student who immediately labels certain materials as trash must be given a hearing and not ridiculed. Before the course is over, however, that student must come to recognize that such an assessment is based on a personal value system that quite likely is not universally held. One person's trash is another's treasure, according to the garage sales crowd and the Library Bill of Rights.

What activities should actually comprise the course and how much time each should receive have been thoroughly enumerated and analyzed by Kingsbury, so that detailed repetition seems unnecessary.[16] A brief overview will suffice.

In the ideal young adult course, students will read a great many print materials in various formats mirroring developmental characteristics of adolescence and covering current topics. Some of the materials will offend or depress, either through their subject matter or style or quality of writing. Students need to assess the appeals of the materials and face straightaway the collection development dilemma of quality versus popularity and the reader's advisory function of recommending recreational as well as instructional materials. They also need practice booktalking both formally and informally. Multimedia materials for viewing and listening should elicit an understanding of the varying potentials of different formats for programming or for getting a message across to a group of users who might miss it in a print medium. The issue of whether all teenagers deserve library service even if the library has to take it to them must be considered. Perhaps even more important, students must understand the "Free Access to Libraries for Minors" interpretation of the *Library Bill of Rights* (adopted by ALA Council, July 1, 1981),[17] and decide whether they really believe in free access to minors with all its implications for future conflicts in real world situations. Some research needs to be encountered, whether in relation to reading preferences or motivations, characteristics of adolescents, management, or a topic of interest to young adults. If possible, students need to produce something they can share. Examples are the *YA Hotline*, a newsletter written and illustrated by Larry Amey's students at Dalhousie University, or mini-booklists/bookmarks like those produced by Patsy Perritt's Louisiana State University class in cooperation with the public library's young adult librarian.

The last word on the role of the library school in the education of the young adult specialist must be a disclaimer. Even under absolutely ideal circumstances, there is no way to teach all that one needs to know. An MLS program really only gets people ready to become good librarians. Informal and continuing education is the responsibility of practitioners and their library administrators, though alumni can certainly encourage library schools to enter in as partners or consultants to the process. Continuing to learn or in the language of systems theory, to process new information is what keeps both personal and organizational systems open, and open systems are the only ones with a chance of survival.

Notes

1. *American Libraries* 13, no. 8 (September 1982): 492.
2. Ibid.
3. Carol L. Learmont and Stephen Van Houten, "Placements and Salaries 1981: Still Holding," *Library Journal*, October 1, 1982, pp. 1821–1823.
4. "Salaries and Placements, 1966," *The Bowker Annual* (New York: Bowker, 1968), pp. 329–331.
5. David Easton, *A Systems Analysis of Political Life* (New York: Wiley, 1965), p. 32.
6. Richard H. Hall, *Organizations: Structure and Process*, 2d ed. (Englewood Cliffs, N.J.: Prentice-Hall, 1977), p. 63.
7. Mary Kingsbury, "How Library Schools Evaluate Faculty Performance," *Journal of Education for Librarianship* 22, no. 4 (Spring 1982): 223.
8. Shirley Fitzgibbons, "Research on Library Services for Children and Young Adults: Implications for Practice," *Emergency Librarian* 9, no. 5 (May–June 1982): 6–17.
9. Susan Steinfirst, "Education of the Young Adult Librarian," in *Libraries and Young Adults*, ed. JoAnn V. Rogers (Littleton, Colo.: Libraries Unlimited, 1979), pp. 145–147.
10. Jean Roos, "Training for Library Service with Young People," *Library Journal*, September 15, 1930, pp. 722–723.
11. "Young Adults Deserve the Best: Competencies for Librarians Serving Youth," *School Library Journal* 29, no. 1 (September 1982): 51.
12. Learmont and Van Houten, op. cit., p. 1827.
13. Steinfirst, op. cit., p. 147.
14. L. J. Amey, comp. and ed., *Course Outlines for Young Adult Literature* (Halifax, N.S.: Dalhousie University School of Library Service, 1982).
15. Mary E. Kingsbury, "Educating Young Adult Librarians: Priorities of Practitioners and Educators," *Drexel Library Quarterly* 14, no. 1 (January 1978): 16.
16. Ibid.
17. *Newsletter on Intellectual Freedom* 30, no. 5 (September 1981): 143–144.

Bibliography

American Library Association, Association for Library Service to Children and Young Adult Services Division. *Selecting Materials for Children and Young Adults*. Chicago, 1980.

————, Young Adult Services Division. *Directions for Library Service to Young Adults.* Chicago, 1977.

————, Young Adult Services Division. *Media and the Young Adult: 1973–1977.* Chicago, 1981.

Bodart, Joni. *Booktalk!* New York: Wilson, 1980.

Books for the Teen Age, 1930– . New York: The Branch Libraries, New York Public Library, 1930– . Annual, published in February.

Braverman, Miriam. *Youth, Society, and the Public Library.* Chicago: American Library Association, 1979.

Carlsen, G. Robert. *Books and the Teenage Reader.* 2d rev. ed. New York: Harper & Row, 1980.

Donelson, Kenneth L., and Alleen Pace Nilsen. *Literature for Today's Young Adults.* Glenview, Ill.: Scott, Foresman, 1980.

Edwards, Margaret A. *The Fair Garden and the Swarm of Beasts.* Rev. and expanded. New York: Hawthorn Books, 1974.

Fader, Daniel. *The New Hooked on Books.* New York: Berkley, 1976.

Lenz, Millicent, and Ramona M. Mahood, comps. *Young Adult Literature: Background and Criticism.* Chicago: American Library Association, 1980.

LiBretto, Ellen V., comp. and ed. *High/Low Handbook.* New York: Bowker, 1981.

16
ALA, YASD, and the Young Adult Librarian

EVELYN SHAEVEL

If service to young adults is to survive, then the librarian who works with young adults must grow up—professionally.

Too often in the past, the young adult librarian, whether working in a public, school, institutional, or alternative type of library service, has been apart from, rather than a part of, the individual library in which she or he worked, or the profession generally. In many cases, this apartness has developed as a means of self-defense. Young adults don't like (don't understand, or can't relate to) the rest of the library staff, and conversely the rest of the staff doesn't understand, can't relate to, or just plain gets nervous around adolescents. Thus, the YA librarian, in an attempt to protect YA patrons, as well as what is classified by many as a unique, specialized, and personalized style of service, will avoid exposing them (both the young adults and the service) to the scrutiny of other staff, or even the administration, by trying to remain anonymous and out of the way. Conversely, the rest of the library staff would often do almost anything to avoid dealing with teenagers; so, to protect themselves from having to deal with what they consider difficult patrons, non-YA librarians are usually thrilled to send anyone between the ages of twelve and eighteen to the YA librarian.

This self-deception and emphasis on personal style have left YA librarians open to charges of disloyalty to organizational goals and of privileged status because of their tendency to ignore or bend institutional rules for their patrons. What is perhaps even worse is that YA librarians have left themselves open to sabotage by fellow staff and termination by administrators. It is time to stop blaming our "endangered species" status solely on inadequate library school preparation and lack of administrative support, because YA services will not survive if YA librarians remain apart from the rest of the library world. YA librarians must enter the mainstream of library service and librarianship by assuming professional responsibilities. They must choose between isolation and involvement, between professional ignorance and professional awareness. And the obvious and only choice for YA librarians who want the young adult to be served—and YA services to survive—is involvement and professional awareness.

Awareness and involvement can take place on many levels, beginning at home with the YA librarian's own job and own library system and covering the continuum through YA services to librarianship on a national level, with involvement in the American Library Association (ALA) and the Young Adult Services Division (YASD). And it should not be done casually or without thought. Talk to people. Let them know who you are, what you are doing, and why. You are a librarian who works with young adults. You don't work in a vacuum; you want young adult services to be considered a vital and essential part of total library service. And one of the best ways for the world (library and nonlibrary) to learn about YA services is for you, an involved and professionally aware YA librarian, to tell them. Service to young adults must not be neglected or ignored!

Local Involvement

Why become involved? Why let people know what is happening in YA services? Library administrators, trustees, and taxpaying parents need to know how valuable and important young adult services are to the library, to youth, and to the community. If the young adult librarian doesn't tell them about the great programs that have been developed, or the unique services given—the work being done with the schools, the joint planning with teachers and school librarians, the class visits, the booktalks, the development of contacts and programs and exchanges of services with other youth-serving professionals, the fact that young adults in the library have produced their own films or literary magazines, and developed their own videogames or computer programs—then it is quite possible that nobody else will. They need to know so that if—and when—the library budget is cut, they will not even consider eliminating or cutting the staff for such a vital, active, and important element of the total library program. And if, perchance, additional funds become available, hopefully they will remember YA services.

Professional awareness at the local level is vitally important for effective YA services. The YA librarian needs to be aware of what is going on throughout the library in order to know how it might affect young adults and library service to them. Let's take a few examples. A revision of the audiovisual circulation policy is being considered. How will it affect access to such AV materials as cassettes, posters, video, and films for the under-sixteen-year-old patrons? A new I&R service is being considered. Does it take into consideration the information and referral needs of adolescents in the areas of birth control, abortion, venereal disease, or sex education? A change is recommended in the library's interlibrary loan service. Does that mean that eighth and ninth graders will not be able to obtain the books they need from the university library to complete their science projects or history research? If at all possible, the YA librarian should take part in formulating policy or developing programs and services for the library. If staff participation isn't encouraged or just isn't possible, at the very least let those who do make policy or plan programs know how their actions or decisions will affect young people. After all, they are the taxpayers and voters of tomorrow.

Getting involved on the local level means working on library staff committees, the ones involved in developing circulation policies or new service programs, or becoming active on the staff association personnel committee, where the issues being considered might be civil service or salary or performance evaluations. There might be wider ranging professional groups outside the library, such as a metropolitan area or countywide library association that meets to discuss library issues. A group of administrators or consultants or age-level specialists might meet to develop workshops, to review publications, or to work out cooperative methods of operation.

Although some of these activities might not seem directly relevant to the immediate needs of the young adult services program, they offer a librarian practical organizational knowledge and experience. Knowing the way in which an organization works and how to effectively use the organizational structure of a group are assets for the young adult librarian who is concerned about and involved in the profession and who wishes to expand a viewpoint beyond the limited perimeters of youth.

Statewide Involvement

Organizational experience on another level may be acquired through involvement in the state library association. In many states, there is a young adult interest group or round table (in some states, it is part of the children's, adult, or school section or interest group), with membership representing a much wider geographic area and often with more experience than local groups. Involvement on a young adult round-table committee or on a state association committee involved in intellectual freedom or professional certification, is an opportunity to make contact with librarians in other areas of library service (and on different rungs of the professional ladder) and to acquire leadership experience.

In Alabama, where no YA round table existed, a group of librarians interested in young adult services held an organizing meeting at a statewide workshop planned by Joan Atkinson of the University of Alabama School of Library Science. As a result of its spring 1976 meeting, an active and viable Young Adult Round Table of the Alabama Library Association was formed. It has put on several regional YA workshops in the state, started a newsletter, and planned a successful preconference.

ALA and YASD

Keeping current on the latest trends and issues within librarianship in general, as well as within the specific field of youth librarianship, is vitally important to the survival of young adult services. Membership in the national professional association, the American Library Association and the Young Adult Services Division can provide a young adult librarian with the information, tools, and program that are necessary to be professionally aware.

YASD, the first step on the professional association ladder, provides the structure through which a young adult librarian may keep current in the areas of materials, service, and programs. Through the years, YASD and its predecessors, including AYPL (Association of Young People's Librarians), have consistently produced tools of the trade for young adult librarians. Basically, these are publications of the division, often produced as projects by a committee of the division or as a result of a conference program.

Top of the News

Top of the News (TON) is the quarterly journal jointly supported by the Association of Library Service to Children (ALSC—formerly CSD) and YASD. *TON* first appeared in 1942 as a small eight-page publication that reported on the activities of the AYPL (whose membership included young adult, children's and school librarians). Since 1942, *TON* has developed into a highly respected professional tool for librarians working with children and young adults. Circulation includes all members of both ALA divisions (about 7,000 people) and almost 2,000 paid subscribers.

Over the years the editors of *TON*—including Margaret Scoggin, Emma Cohn, Johanna Hanson, Sara Fenwick, Dorothy Broderick, Mary Jane Anderson, Caroline Coughlin, Shirley Fitzgibbons, and Audrey Eaglen—have provided a journal reflecting the changing patterns of service to young adults and children. The features and articles in *TON*, especially the theme issues produced under the editorship of Audrey Eaglen, have provided outstanding coverage of subjects and service areas of concern to young adult librarians. Among these theme issues are "Reflections on Fantasy and Science Fiction" (Vol. 39, no. 1, Fall 1982); "Library Services to the Gifted" (Vol. 38, no. 4, Summer 1982); "The World of Book Publishing" (Vol. 38, no. 3, Spring 1982); "Reviews, Reviewing and the Review Media" (Vol. 35, no. 2, Winter 1979); and "Sex and Youth: A Symposium" (Vol. 34, no. 2, Winter 1978).

In 1983 Marilyn Kaye became the new *TON* editor. Kaye's

first two issues will focus on computers and other new technology in relation to library service to youth.

Other divisional publications

As part of its function within the ALA structure, YASD has the specific responsibility to evaluate and promote materials of interest to adolescents. To fulfill this charge, YASD has produced a number of annotated booklists, in pamphlet format, which have proven to be popular and useful tools for anyone who works with, lives with (parents), or deals with teenagers in any way.

The *Best Books for Young Adults* list is selected annually by a YASD committee and published, with annotations, in pamphlet form. The list, which has had several sponsors, has been produced in various forms and under a number of names since it first appeared in 1930, when the School Libraries Section of ALA prepared "Thirty Books for Young People, 1930." Originally the purpose of the list was to point out those new adult books published each year that were considered to be most significant or interesting for young adult readers. Since 1966, when the list assumed its present name, new young adult titles as well as adult books (a distinction made by publishers according to the publishing house department where a title originates) were to be considered by the committee. The basis for selection to the list has become "proven or potential appeal and worth" to young adults.

Selected Films for Young Adults, another annual media evaluation list, first appeared in 1975 and contains films recommended for use in programs for young adults.

The series of lists of Outstanding Books for the College Bound were first produced in 1959 when the National Education Association requested a list for college-bound students. Revised seven times by YASD committees since 1959, the latest edition was published in 1982 when *Outstanding Fiction, Non-Fiction, Biographies and Books for the Performing Arts* appeared. In all, almost a million and a half copies of these lists have been distributed to librarians and college-bound young people over the last twenty-five years.

Other pamphlets produced by YASD include two that meet special needs of select groups of young adults. YASD's *High-Interest, Low-Reading Level Booklist* first appeared in 1980, with a second edition published in 1982. It is expected that this list will be issued annually beginning in 1983. *Libros a Tu Gusto*, a list of books available in Spanish, has had three editions. Other pamphlets or books produced by YASD committees (and published by ALA) include *Look, Listen, Explain: Developing Community Library Service to Young Adults* (1975); *Media and the Young Adult: A Selective Bibliography, 1959–1972* (1977) and *1973–77* (1981); *Book Bait* (1969, 3rd rev. ed. 1979), originally an AYPL project, which was revised by Elinor Walker; *Film Profiles for Youth* (1972, supplement 1973); *Directions for Library Service for Young Adults* (1978), which provides a philosophical statement of what YA services should and can be; and *Selecting Materials for Children and Young Adults: A Bibliography of Bibliographies and Review Sources* (1980), an annotated listing of more than 300 bibliographies and review sources, compiled by a joint committee of YASD and ALSC. *Sex Education for Adolescents: A Bibliography of Low-Cost Materials* (1980) was prepared by a joint committee of YASD, the American Academy of Pediatrics, and Planned Parenthood Federation of America. To help YA librarians develop their own continuing education programs, the YASD Education Committee developed the publication *Cheap CE: Providing Continuing Education with Limited Resources: A Practical Guide* (YASD, 1981), by Linda Waddle, which offers step-by-step suggestions for selecting a topic, planning details, making local arrangements, and evaluating the activities.

Other tangible tools in somewhat unique form have included "Young Adult Programming Ideas (YAPI)," originally called "Living Library Patterns," which was a collection of ideas, outlines, fliers, bibliographies, and evaluations, gathered together in a box and routed around the country; the YASD *Survival Kit*, which includes original items as well as materials from libraries around the country, all of which demonstrate the purpose and methods of providing services to young adults; and information packets on topics such as "Intellectual Freedom and the Rights of Youth" and "High-Interest, Low-Reading Level Materials."

Conference programs

Each year, YASD organizes, plans, and presents programs during the ALA annual conference. The ALA annual conference itself provides all librarians with an unequaled opportunity for continuing library education through the myriad and diverse programs scheduled over a five- to six-day period and covering every area of librarianship, from management, technical services, and research to reference and automation. Among the annual conference continuing education programs that YASD has presented in the last decade and a half are "Intellectual Freedom and the Teenager" (San Francisco, 1967), as a result of which the word "age" was incorporated into Article V of the *Library Bill of Rights*; "The Young Adult in the Media World" (Dallas, 1971), which was concerned with ways to integrate AV equipment and materials into traditional library programs and resulted in the publication of *Mixed-Means Programming with Young Adults*; "Book You" (San Francisco, 1975), a reevaluation of the "Best Books" lists of the previous fifteen years, which resulted in *Still Alive: The Best of the Best, 1960–74*; "Sexism in Adolescent Lives and Literature" (San Francisco, 1975); "Librarian as Youth Counselor" (Detroit, 1977); "Paperback Power: How to Get It" (Detroit, 1977), which inspired the paperback theme issue of *TON* (Autumn 1977); "Dispelling the High-Low Blues" (Chicago, 1978), a two-day preconference sponsored by YASD and ALSC, which provided participants with training on locating, evaluating, and using high-low materials and resulted in the first YASD *High-Interest, Low-Reading Level Booklist*; and "Research: The How and Why of It" (New York, 1980), a preconference sponsored by YASD/ALSC/PLA. Other 1980 programs covered topics such as film censorship, popular culture, and adult trade books for young adults; 1981 took ALA to San Francisco where YASD programs focused on research, specialized publishing, and "Television, Books and the Young Reader." "Booktalking: Basic Skills and Beyond," a preconference, began the events in Philadelphia (1982), followed by programs on lobbying for youth and youth participation in library decision making.

Over the years, YASD has also provided its conference attendees with opportunities to meet authors who are popular with teenagers, including Judy Blume, Robert Cormier, Richard Peck, Anne McCaffrey, Jamake Highwater, M. E. Kerr, and Stephen King.

*Other ways a professional
association helps*

With the assistance of YASD, the staff at ALA headquarters provides advisory and referral services in all areas of young adult materials and services, ranging from collection development, programming, intellectual freedom, and establishment of YA services to school and public library relations, rights of the young, and YA staff development. A telephone call or letter is all that is needed for *anyone*, ALA/YASD member or not, to avail him- or herself of the expertise of the ALA headquarters staff and its resources.

ALA, through the Young Adult Services Division, also provides YA librarians with an opportunity to meet with librarians in other specialties on an equal footing. Through ALA/YASD, the YA librarian can discuss the inadequacies of library education in terms of young adult librarianship with the deans and faculty of library schools; the problems due to the lack of hard statistical data concerning the use of public libraries by teenagers can be faced by library administrators and YA librarians together; or programs in which school and public librarians might work more cooperatively might develop.

Through conference programs, YASD provides YA librarians with an opportunity to meet the authors and publishers of young adult literature and the creators, producers, and distributors of audiovisual materials, so that they might discuss their mutual concerns, the improvement of materials for young adults and easier and more effective methods of distribution of these materials. YASD provides speakers and materials for local, state, and regional library association meetings. It also is working to develop models for young adult services workshops, which can then be used as prototypes by other groups around the country.

A primary objective of YASD is to establish liaisons on the national level with other organizations of youth-service professionals such as Planned Parenthood Federation of America, National Council of Teachers of English, Adolescent Literature Assembly of NCTE, Society for Adolescent Medicine, Girl Scouts, National Youth Alternatives Projects, and American Youth Hostels, among others. YASD is attempting to develop patterns of working together and potential programs with these groups, which may then be further developed and refined for use at the local level.

Ultimately, YASD sees as one of its primary responsibilities to advocate YA services as a viable and respected component within the profession. A strong, united group of aware and involved young adult librarians expressing views on issues of importance to youth and youth librarianship cannot be ignored.

Continuing education and support

As budgets are reduced and less money and attention are paid to providing services to teenagers, and as less training and support are given to young adult librarians, the activities, publications, and programs of the Young Adult Services Division become even more important. YASD continues to be a source of support for YA librarians and library service to young adults by playing a strong role in the professional development and training of librarians as well as serving as an advocate for library services to adolescents on the national level.

The programs, publications, and services offered by YASD cover topics and provide expertise in areas that are often not possible to cover in local situations. The Young Adult Services Division of ALA continues to advocate library service to young adults and support the staff providing these services. In return, librarians who work with youth must support the professional association, both actively and financially.

17
The Leadership of the State Library Agency in Young Adult Services

BRUCE DANIELS

During the 1980s, state agencies, when working in the area of young adult services, will have to look at the total context of library services in the state. With the introduction of library automation and the new communication technology, services to the various age levels have become more interconnected and dependent upon each other. Resource sharing and network development, without which libraries would not have sufficient access to information to satisfy user needs, have made it essential to determine the impact of a local development on other parts of the state. No longer can local services be viewed in isolation.

The state library agency is in a unique position to provide the strong leadership required for such developments to occur and to be sustained over an extended period of time. Its power to influence library development is derived from both state and federal legislation. Most state library laws give the state library agency sole responsibility for the development of library services to citizens of the state. In addition, the Library Services and Construction Act designates the state library agency responsible for administering federal funds for library development and cooperation.

Many state library agencies use standards as a means to foster library development. For an individual library to receive state funding it would be required to provide certain levels of service and to operate under accepted administrative procedures. As related to young adult services, for example, the Rhode Island Department of State Library Services, in recently revised public library standards, requires local public libraries:

To provide young adults and children access to all materials;

To provide and promote interlibrary loan service to users of all ages; and

To allocate 5% to 10% of its materials budget to young adult materials.[1]

Furthermore, in the accompanying guidelines, it is strongly suggested that local libraries:

Schedule visits to classes in elementary, junior high and senior high schools at least once a year; and

Offer services specifically designed for pre-school children, elementary-age children, and young adults.[2]

By setting realistic standards for local libraries, the state library agency is ensured that library users have access to at least minimal level of service, which may not otherwise have been provided.

Long-range planning by the state library agency also significantly affects library development. In order to receive Library Services and Construction Act funds, every state library agency is required to develop a five-year plan, which libraries throughout the state use for guidance in their planning efforts and in developing proposals for demonstration projects. Involving as large a part of the library community as possible in the planning process, either on the planning committee or in providing testimony, can contribute to the library community's awareness of certain issues or problems of concern to the state.

The Roles of the State Library Agency

The basic function of any state library agency is that of a change agent. As demands and needs of users shift and services to the community have to be modified to reflect the changes, the agency assumes one of three roles—adviser, facilitator, or catalyst.

Serving as an adviser is the least active role. An agency consultant listens to a particular problem and suggests various solutions. It is the client, however, who determines the final plan of action.

In the role of facilitator, the state library agency becomes more active. A problem or a situation is identified, usually involving more than one institution or community, and an agency convenes a meeting of the interested individuals for the purpose of resolving the situation or bringing about a desired change. The consultant assists the group by clarifying issues and making sure that everyone concerned understands the proposed results and is comfortable with them. Members of the group are responsible for implementing the changes.

The most active role for the state library agency is that of a catalyst. An agency consultant identifies a particular problem or recognizes the need for change and develops strategies or initiates a process that will bring about the desired change. In this case, the agency is directly responsible for bringing about the change.

Administration

As financial support becomes more constrained and accountability to funding sources more stringent, state library agencies must give the administrative area higher priority. Most young adult librarians have only minimal administrative experience, and without sound administration for all levels of services, institutions will not survive.

The key element is planning, both short term and long range. A long-range plan would include information on assessing needs, developing goals and objectives, establishing strategies, setting priorities, developing evaluative measures, and integrating the plan into the total library plan. With a view of not only what is happening throughout the state but the region and nation as well, an agency consultant is able to offer various alternatives in dealing with a particular issue that a library staff member might not be able to offer and to suggest subject experts who could be contacted for additional information.

Using the data collected from the planning process, the state library agency can assist the young adult librarian to develop an advocacy strategy. It is most vital to convince the library director of the need for strong support of young adult services. A community advocacy group composed of young adults and youth workers can also be formed with the agency's help. In setting up a staff development program, the state library agency can assist the young adult librarian with needs assessment and interpretation of the data. The results of the assessment will determine whether there is a need for an individualized program or a statewide program. An agency consultant can assist in obtaining the appropriate workshop leaders and serve as an observer during workshop sessions, providing continuous feedback to the workshop leader and planners.

Materials

The state library agency must assume a strong advocacy role to ensure that young adult needs are addressed by local book selection policies and collection development plans. Through periodic field visits to the local library by an agency consultant, or, if that is not possible, through regular written communication, workshops or seminars, and incentive grants, the state library agency must make library directors aware of the importance of providing for young adult needs.

The state library agency also must take an active role in providing local libraries access to materials for review purposes. In smaller geographic areas, a materials review center can be established at the state library. In areas of greater size, large libraries can be contracted to provide the service. Committees should be established to review materials and to prepare selection lists, through which young adult librarians, who might not otherwise have such an opportunity, can gain experience in evaluating materials.

The state library agency can assist libraries without young

adult librarians and collections in meeting the needs of young adults. In Rhode Island, for example, the Department of State Library Services established rotating collections of young adult paperbacks purchased with federal funds. Participating libraries retain the collection for a period of three months. The success of this project, as evidenced by a substantial waiting list for the collections, has demonstrated to library directors that the need for such materials exists and has shown how the library can respond to meet this need. Some libraries, as a result, have purchased more paperbacks. This method could very easily be used to provide videocassettes and computer programs.

Microcomputer software, an area that has developed very quickly, has great potential for young adults. Schools are successfully introducing microcomputers into their curriculum, and as a result young adults are more familiar with the uses and the capabilities of microcomputers than are adults. But at a time when libraries are facing difficult financial conditions, few libraries have been able to respond. Out of economic necessity, the state library agency will have to assume a strong role in this area. It can establish review committees to examine the computer software and disseminate their findings. It also can establish rotating collections of software for libraries to use.

Potential does exist to resolve the fundamental problem— the acquisition of the microcomputer. State governments are beginning to recognize the necessity for the education system to prepare people to use computer and related technology. In Rhode Island, the governor has developed a proposal to provide microcomputers for all of the state's schools, and the Department of State Library Services is developing a proposal to include public libraries in the project. The U.S. Congress, which is also examining the problem, is expected to develop legislation that will provide some funding for the acquisition of microcomputers.

The state library agency also must take a leadership role in combating censorship. Before censorship problems arise, librarians must know how to build strong community support for intellectual freedom principles. They also need to learn various techniques to deal with individuals who challenge the library's action. Finally, the state library agency must give its moral support to a library and its staff when a censorship case does occur.

Programming

It is in programming that the state library agency assumes most dramatically the three roles described earlier. For the librarian who wants an objective reaction to plans for programming activities the state library agency can serve as adviser. This is especially important in areas where there are few young adult librarians with whom to exchange views and to provide feedback. Additionally, the state library agency can provide advice on how to resolve problems encountered in developing a particular program and can offer the names of resource people, agencies, or organizations that might be able to help.

The agency also is in a position to be able to identify a situation or a trend on a statewide basis. An example of this is deinstitutionalization. Libraries need to develop a service program to meet the special needs of the increasing number of developmentally disabled young adults who are living in group homes or with parents. The state library agency can assemble a group composed of library directors, young adult librarians, insitutional librarians, and other institutional staff to discuss the needs of these users, the best way to serve them, and how to implement services at the local level.

With primary responsibility for long-range planning in the state, the state library agency is also the catalyst for developing new programs or services that will achieve the goals and objectives of the plan. An example of this might be the development of young adult programming on cable television. The state library agency can develop a basic framework for beginning such a project and make several initial contacts to assess the feasibility of the idea. Then a committee of young adult librarians, school librarians, media specialists, and cable company representatives can be formed to develop the project. When the planning is completed, implementation work can be started at the local level, and the state library agency can assume the role of an adviser to the young adult librarian and the local committee.

Grant Proposal Development

It is apparent that local public funding for library and information services will not substantially increase in the 1980s. To fund new and innovative services libraries will have to rely on what will probably be insignificant federal funds and on foundation funding. The state library agency can play a vital role in obtaining funds for both local and statewide projects.

On the local level, it can advise the young adult librarian on how to obtain grant funding—how to find out what foundations provide funds for specific projects. In addition, it can critique grant proposals and offer suggestions on strengthening them. For projects that may not be appropriate for funding by large foundations, the agency can suggest possible local funding sources such as McDonalds or Waldenbooks and ways to approach them.

The initiative to establish a committee to develop a grant proposal for a statewide project should come from the state library agency. (A prime source of funding for statewide projects could be the Youth Grant Program of the National Endowment for the Humanities.) Once a draft of the proposal is completed, it is the responsibility of the state library agency to explain the proposal to young adult librarians and library directors, elicit comments and suggestions, and keep them informed of developments as the proposal is refined and submitted to funding sources.

Because many states use Library Services and Construction Act funds to support demonstration projects, it is essential for the state library agency to convince libraries to develop proposals for young adult services projects. The agency can then serve as an adviser to the public libraries that want to develop proposals.

Public Relations

Assistance from the state library agency to librarians wanting to promote young adult activities can be in the form of suggestions as to the best ways of publicizing a particular activity, or it can be the duplicating of fliers describing the activity.

On the state level, the state library agency, working with the state library association, the state educational media association, the state chapter of the National Education Association, or the American Federation of Teachers, can develop a statewide campaign promoting young adult services. The campaign can include radio and television spot announcements, newspaper publicity, and participation on television talk shows. To assist local young adult librarians, a press package can be developed for use with local newspapers and radio stations, and the agency can attempt to obtain the assistance of a noted local sports or television celebrity.

Another idea is a campaign to promote library services to young adults, such as a statewide videofilm competition. Each local library sponsors a competition and submits the winning entry to the state library agency. The top ten videofilms can be made available to local libraries for showing.

Resource Sharing

By being responsible for promoting and coordinating resource sharing on a statewide basis, the state library agency is in a pivotal position to assess the strengths and weaknesses of a particular type of service. For example, it can assist libraries in developing plans to strengthen their materials collections. It also can monitor the policies and procedures for a resource-sharing agreement to ensure that all individuals have access to materials and information—a role that becomes more important as the use of computer technology increases. Given the limited resources and the communication technology that libraries will have available during the 1980s, state library agencies must act now to ensure young adults the full advantage of the opportunities that exist in resource sharing. In many locations young adults do not have access to such resource-sharing activities as data-base searching and interlibrary loan service. Because state library agencies coordinate interlibrary loan activities, they can take steps to ensure that young adults have the opportunity to use interlibrary loan. For example, in Rhode Island, the Department of State Library Services requires local libraries to provide and promote interlibrary loan service to all age groups.

The state library agency also can undertake activities to promote cooperation between public and school libraries at the local level. In Rhode Island, the agency worked together with the state Department of Education to develop guidelines that detailed cooperative projects in the areas of communication, resource sharing, skill sharing, and programming. Unfortunately, before the guidelines could be finalized, the school library consultant's position was abolished due to federal funding reductions.

To reinforce school and public library cooperation, the

Rhode Island Department of State Library Services established the Young Adult Round Table. At meetings of the round table, librarians review new materials and discuss ways to better serve young adults. Through these meetings a strong relationship has developed between school and public librarians throughout the state.

Training

With the fiscal contraints that local libraries will encounter in the 1980s, funds for attendance at workshops and national conferences will no longer be available. The state library agency must assume responsibility to develop ongoing continuing education programs, if librarians within the state are to keep abreast of new developments within the library profession. Two particular areas that will undoubtedly have to be addressed in any state's continuing education program are technology and local continuing education activities. Young adult librarians will need to understand fully technological advancements to make sure that young adults will be able to utilize the technology to its fullest extent.

A staff development program also is essential at the local level, in order for the young adult librarian to keep other staff members aware of new trends in young adult services. Activities can include speakers from social agencies discussing ways of working with young adults and problems that arise or speakers discussing new youth programs in the community. Over a period of time, staff development activities can reduce the fears and anxieties that staff may have in interacting with young adults. As the young adult librarian is planning the staff development program, an agency consultant can serve as an adviser, critiquing the program, making suggestions, or providing the names of individuals who could serve as resource people for particular programs.

The Young Adult Consultant

State agency consultants are an important element in strengthening library services. They assist library staffs and boards of trustees in assessing the needs of their communities, in evaluating the effectiveness of existing services, and in making changes in services to more effectively meet community needs. At the same time, they can assess the continuing education needs of the state and develop an ongoing continuing education program.

The greatest disagreement in the profession regarding the state library agency's role in young adult services is whether the state library agency should have a young adult consultant on its staff or whether it should contract with a public library to provide this service. Many maintain that it is essential for a consultant to maintain day-to-day contact with the user group. Without such interaction, it is felt that the consultant will no longer be aware of usage trends and the user group's interests. The general impression is that the advice from the practitioner is more reliable than that given by a consultant from the state library agency.

There are a number of problems with that point of view. If the individual is responsible for providing user services, the direct service will have to be the top priority. For instance, during staff shortages the young adult librarian may be required to assist in other departments. Consulting services would have to be diminished and, as a result, statewide development and coordination would be severely affected.

Problems can arise in implementing state library agency policies and programs if the consultant is employed by another institution. The consultant must follow the directives of superiors. If the library in which the consultant is employed is in serious conflict with the state library agency, the consultant undoubtedly would find it difficult to represent effectively the interests of the state library agency.

To have effective consulting services, it is essential for the state library agency to employ the young adult consultant. There are no user service demands upon the individual, so the consultant's efforts are totally committed to advising library staffs. It is much easier for this individual to attend conferences and workshops. Involvement in library association activity is also more possible.

The structure for young adult services in state library agencies varies widely. In Rhode island, a committee consisting of the supervisor of adult services and two institutional consultants, who work with institutionalized youth, do the basic planning for the Young Adult Round Table meeting. The programs for the monthly meetings are planned by the participants. Individual consulting requests are handled by the supervisor of adult services or the supervisor of young readers' services. There is also a cadre of individuals who provide consultant services.

Only two states—Hawaii and North Carolina—have young adult consultants on the state library agency staff. Some states, such as Missouri, Ohio, Oklahoma, and Vermont, assign the responsibility to children's consultants. Other states have general consultants providing the young adult services. Because so few states currently have a young adult consultant, it is not realistic to think that this will change in the near future given the present economic situation. However, the ideal remains that one day there will be a young adult consultant on each state library agency's staff.

Notes

1. Rhode Island Department of State Library Services, *Standards for Rhode Island Public Libraries* (Providence, 1983), pp. 15 and 21.

2. Ibid., p. 17

Appendix I
Guidelines for Youth Participation in Library Decision Making

Prepared by the Committee on Youth Participation in Library Decision Making of the Young Adult Services Division of the American Library Association in cooperation with the National Commission on Resources for Youth for the YASD President's Program, ALA Conference, Philadelphia, July 1982.

WHAT:

Youth participation in libraries is involvement of young adults in responsible action and significant decision making which affects the design and delivery of library and information services for their peers and the community.

WHY:

Youth participation in library decision making is important as a means of achieving more responsive and effective library and information service for this age group. It is even more important as an experience through which young adults can enhance their learning, personal development, citizenship, and transition to adulthood.

Reprinted by permission of the Young Adult Services Division, American Library Association.

HOW:

Youth participation in library decision making requires that adults (librarians, administrators, members of governing and advisory bodies) recognize that young adults can make a positive contribution, and that adults respect the right of young adults to participate in decisions on matters that affect them.

Projects involving youth should have the following characteristics:

be centered on issues of real interest and concern to youth

have the potential to benefit people other than those directly involved

allow for youth input from the planning stage forward

focus on some specific, doable tasks

receive adult support and guidance, but avoid adult domination

allow for learning and development of leadership and group work skills

contain opportunities for training and for discussion of progress made and problems encountered

give evidence of youth decisions being implemented

avoid exploitation of youth for work which benefits the agency rather than the young adults

seek to recruit new participants on a regular basis

plan for staff time, funds, administrative support, transportation, etc., before launching project

show promise of becoming an ongoing, long-term activity

Appendix II
Competencies for Librarians Serving Youth

Prepared by the Education Committee of the Young Adult Services Division of the American Library Association, this list was developed as a guideline for library educators in identifying competencies that librarians working with young adults in any type of information agency should be able to demonstrate.

Area I: Leadership and Professionalism

The student will be able to:
1. Develop and demonstrate leadership skills in articulating a program of excellence for young adults.
2. Exhibit planning and evaluating skills in the development of a comprehensive program for young adults.
3. Develop and demonstrate a commitment to professionalism.
   a. Adhere to the American Library Association Code of Ethics.
   b. Demonstrate a non-judgmental attitude toward young adults.
   c. Preserve confidentiality in interactions with young adults.

Reprinted by permission of the American Library Association, "Competencies for Librarians Serving Youth," prepared by the Young Adult Services Division of American Library Association, copyright ©1982.

4. Plan for personal and professional growth and career development through active participation in professional associations and continuing education.
5. Develop and demonstrate a strong commitment to the right of young adults to have access to information, consistent with the American Library Association's *Library Bill of Rights*.
6. Demonstrate an understanding of and a respect for diversity in cultural and ethnic values.
7. Encourage young adults to become lifelong library users by helping them to discover what libraries have to offer and how to use libraries.

Area II: Knowledge of Client Group

The student will be able to:
1. Apply factual and interpretative information on adolescent psychology, growth and development, sociology, and popular culture in planning for materials and services for young adults.
2. Apply knowledge of the reading process and of types of reading problems in the development of the collection and program for young adults.
3. Identify the special needs of discrete groups of young adults and design and implement programs and build collections appropriate to their needs.

Area III: Communication

The student will be able to:
1. Demonstrate effective interpersonal relations with young adults, administrators, other professionals who work with young adults, and the community by:
   a. using principles of group dynamics and group process.
   b. establishing regular channels of communication (both written and oral) with each group.
2. Apply principles of effective communication which reinforce positive behaviors in young adults.

Area IV: Administration

A. Planning

The student will be able to:
1. Formulate goals, objectives, and methods of evaluation for a young adult program based on determined needs.
   a. Design and conduct a community analysis and needs assessment.
   b. Apply research findings for the development and improvement of the young adult program.
   c. Design, conduct, and evaluate local action research for program improvement.

2. Design, implement, and evaluate an ongoing public relations and report program directed toward young adults, administrators, boards, staff, other agencies serving young adults, and the community at large.
3. Identify and cooperate with other information agencies in networking arrangements to expand access to information for young adults.
4. Develop, justify, administer, and evaluate a budget for the young adult program.
5. Develop physical facilities which contribute to the achievement of young adult program goals.

B. Managing

The student will be able to:

1. Supervise and evaluate other staff members.
2. Design, implement, and evaluate an ongoing program of staff development.
3. Develop policies and procedures for the efficient operation of all technical functions (including acquisition, processing, circulation, collection maintenance, equipment supervision, and scheduling of young adult programs).
4. Identify external sources of funding and other support and apply for those suitable for the young adult program.
5. Monitor legislation and judicial decisions pertinent to young adults, especially those which affect youth rights, and disseminate this information.

Area V: Knowledge of Materials

The student will be able to:

1. Formulate a selection policy for young adult materials, consistent with the parent institution's selection policy, with a systematic procedure for handling challenges.
2. Develop a materials collection for young adults which includes all appropriate formats, using a broad range of selection sources.
3. Demonstrate a knowledge and appreciation of literature for young adults.
4. Identify current reading, viewing, and listening interests of young adults and incorpoate these findings into collection development and programs.
5. Design and locally produce materials in a variety of formats to expand the collections.
6. Incorporate technological advances (e.g., computers, video) in the library program.

Area VI: Access to Information

The student will be able to:
1. Organize collections to guarantee easy access to information.

2. Use current standard methods of cataloging and classification, and be aware of the newest technology.
3. Create an environment which attracts and invites young adults to use the collection.
4. Develop special tools which provide access to information not readily available, e.g., community resources, special collections.
5. Devise and publicize pathfinders, book lists, displays, etc., which will ease access to collections and will motivate use.

Area VII: Services

The student will be able to:
1. Utilize a variety of techniques (e.g., booktalking, discussion) to encourage use of materials.
2. Provide a variety of information services (e.g., information referral, crisis intervention counseling, on-line data bases) to meet the diverse needs of young adults.
3. Instruct young adults in the basic information gathering and research skills needed for current and future use.
4. Encourage young adults in the use of all types of materials for their personal growth and enjoyment.
5. Design, implement, and evaluate specific programs and activities (both in the library and in the community) for young adults, based on their needs and interests.
6. Involve young adults in planning and implementing services for their age group.

Index